Cambridge IGCSE®
English as a Second Language

Practice Tests 1

Tom Bradbury and Mark Fountain

Series editors: Katia Carter and Tim Carter

CAMBRIDGE
UNIVERSITY PRESS

CAMBRIDGE
UNIVERSITY PRESS

University Printing House, Cambridge CB2 8BS, United Kingdom

One Liberty Plaza, 20th Floor, New York, NY 10006, USA

477 Williamstown Road, Port Melbourne, VIC 3207, Australia

314–321, 3rd Floor, Plot 3, Splendor Forum, Jasola District Centre
New Delhi – 110025, India

79 Anson Road, #06–04/06, Singapore 079906

Cambridge University Press is part of the University of Cambridge.

It furthers the University's mission by disseminating knowledge in the pursuit of education, learning and research at the highest international levels of excellence.

Information on this title: www.cambridge.org/9781108546102

© Cambridge University Press 2018

First published 2018

20 19 18 17 16 15 14 13 12 11 10 9 8 7 6 5 4 3 2

Printed in the United Kingdom by Latimer Trend

A catalogue record for this publication is available from the British Library

ISBN 978-1-108-54610-2
Paperback (with answers)

ISBN 978-1-108-54611-9
Paperback (without answers)

....

Contents

Cambridge IGCSE® English as a Second Language – introduction to the exam

The Cambridge IGCSE® English as a Second Language exam is an international exam for speakers whose first language isn't English. The exam is mainly for learners who are between 14 and 16 years old and who have been studying for the exam for two years. It is recommended that learners have completed approximately 130 guided learning hours before entering for the exam. However, the number of hours may vary depending on the proficiency of each learner at the start of the course.

There are two levels, Core and Extended. The Core level is aimed at learners who have reached at least high intermediate level (B1+). The Extended level is for learners who are at least at an upper-intermediate level (B2). Core candidates are awarded grades C–G while extended candidates can gain grades A*–E. All the examination-style papers in this book are Extended level. They are, of course, excellent practice for Core candidates too.

There are two syllabuses 0510 and 0511. The content of these syllabuses is identical. However, candidates who are entered for the 0510 syllabus (Speaking endorsement) are given a separate grade for their performance in the speaking component. Candidates who are entered for the 0511 syllabus (Count-in speaking) are given one grade for all three components: reading and writing, listening and speaking.

Syllabus 0510 (Speaking endorsement)

Reading and writing component:	Listening component:	Speaking component:
counts towards 70% of the final grade	counts towards 30% of the final grade	a separate grade is given

Syllabus 0511 (Count-in speaking)

Reading and writing component:	Listening component:	Speaking component:
counts towards 60% of the final grade	counts towards 20% of the final grade	counts towards 20% of the final grade

© Cambridge University Press 2018

Exam overview

Reading and Writing paper*					
Exercises	Assessment objectives tested	Extended paper (2 hours)	Number of marks awarded (80 marks)	Core paper (1 hour and 30 minutes)	Number of marks awarded (60 marks)
Exercise 1	R1	Reading comprehension for specific detail	13 marks	Reading comprehension for specific detail	9 marks
Exercise 2	R1, R2, R3, R4	Multiple matching	10 marks	Multiple matching	8 marks
Exercise 3	R1, R2, R3	Note-making	9 marks	Note-making	7 marks
Exercise 4	R1, R2, R3, W1, W2, W3, W4	Summary writing	16 marks	Summary writing	12 marks
Exercise 5	W1, W2, W3, W4, W5	Extended writing (informal email)	16 marks	Extended writing (informal email)	12 marks
Exercise 6	W1, W2, W3, W4, W5	Discursive writing (review, report or article)	16 marks	Discursive writing (review, report, article)	12 marks

* Candidates are not allowed to use dictionaries.

Listening paper**					
Exercises	Assessment objectives tested	Extended paper (50 minutes)	Number of marks awarded (40 marks)	Core paper (40 minutes)	Number of marks awarded (30 marks)
Exercise 1 (Question 1–4)	L1	Four short extracts, listening for specific detail (informal or semi-formal dialogues, announcements, monologues)	8 marks	Four short extracts, listening for specific detail	8 marks
Exercise 2 (Question 5)	L1, L2	Gap-filling (formal talk)	8 marks	Gap-filling (formal talk)	8 marks
Exercise 3 (Question 6)	L3, L4	Multiple matching (informal monologues)	6 marks	Multiple matching	6 marks
Exercise 4 (Question 7)	L3, L4	Multiple choice (semi-formal interview)	8 marks	Multiple choice (semi-formal interview)	8 marks
Exercise 5 (Question 8 part a)	L1, L2, L3, L4	Gap-filling (formal talk)	5 marks	N/A	N/A
Exercise 5 (Question 8 part b)	L1, L2, L3, L4	Gap-filling (informal conversation)	5 marks	N/A	N/A

** Each part of the listening paper is played twice

   © Cambridge University Press 2018

Speaking paper***				
Parts	**Assessment objectives tested**	**Core and Extended (10–15 minutes)**	**What happens**	**Number of marks awarded (30 marks)**
Part A	N/A	Welcome	The examiner welcomes the candidate and explains the procedure.	N/A
Part B	N/A	Warm-up (2–3 minutes)	The examiner asks the candidate questions about their life outside school, and interests, to put candidates at ease. For example: *What do you enjoy doing in your free time?, What are your favourite hobbies, and why?, What are your plans for the weekend?*, etc. The questions should not focus on exam preparation or school studies. This part is not assessed.	N/A
Part C	N/A	Preparation (2–3 minutes)	The candidate reads the topic card selected by the examiner and thinks about what to say about each of the five prompts on the card. The candidate isn't allowed to write anything down, but can ask the examiner for clarification on any unknown vocabulary. The candidate must use the whole time allocated for this part of the test.	N/A
Part D	S1, S2, S3, S4, S5	Conversation (6–9 minutes)	The examiner and the candidate have a conversation about the five ideas/bullet points on the topic card. All five bullet points should be covered during the conversation in the order given on the topic card. The examiner asks extra questions on the topic to help the conversation to develop. This part mustn't be a monologue by the candidate, but a two-way conversation. This is the only part that is assessed.	30 marks

*** The whole of the speaking exam is recorded including the preparation part. The speaking exam is conducted by one examiner who may be also the teacher. The candidates are examined individually, **not** in pairs. The examiner and the candidate must speak English throughout the whole exam.

Assessment objectives

Reading

R1 identify and select relevant information
R2 understand ideas, opinions and attitudes
R3 show understanding of the connections between ideas, opinions and attitudes
R4 understand what is implied but not directly stated, e.g. gist, writer's purpose, intention and feelings

Writing

W1 communicate information/ideas/opinions clearly, accurately and effectively
W2 organise ideas into coherent paragraphs using a range of appropriate linking devices
W3 use a range of grammatical structures and vocabulary accurately and effectively
W4 show control of punctuation and spelling
W5 use appropriate register and style/format for the given purpose and audience

Listening

L1 identify and select relevant information
L2 understand ideas, opinions and attitudes
L3 show understanding of the connections between ideas, opinions and attitudes
L4 understand what is implied but not directly stated, e.g. gist, speaker's purpose, intention and feelings

Speaking

S1 communicate ideas/opinions clearly, accurately and effectively
S2 develop responses and link ideas using a range of appropriate linking devices
S3 use a range of grammatical structures and vocabulary accurately and effectively
S4 show control of pronunciation and intonation patterns
S5 engage in a conversation and contribute effectively to help move the conversation forward

Assessment criteria for writing and speaking

The following criteria are designed to help you and your students when grading oral and written work. We have simplified the grading criteria used by Cambridge Assessment International Education in the Cambridge IGCSE English as a Second Language exam, so that they are accessible for students to understand success criteria.

If you wish to see the official grade criteria for Cambridge IGCSE English as a Second Language, please visit the Cambridge Assessment International Education website.

Writing

Give a separate Content mark and Language mark by deciding which band is the best fit for each. (The Content and Language marks can be very different if necessary.) If all of the criteria of the band are met, give the upper mark; if it meets some of the criteria, give the lower mark. If the writing is very short in Exercise 5 or 6 (below 105 words), deduct 1 or 2 marks.

The top mark for extended candidates is 8 for both content and language. The top mark for core candidates is 6 for both content and language.

Exercise 4

Mark	Content (maximum 8 marks)	Mark	Language (maximum 8 marks)
7–8	• Includes 7–8 content points • All content in the summary is relevant to the task	7–8	• Content points in the summary are organised very well • Appropriate linking words/phrases are used clearly to connect ideas • The summary is written using own words as much as possible • Almost no errors in vocabulary and grammar
5–6	• Includes 5–6 content points • Most content in the summary is relevant to the task	5–6	• Content points in the summary are well organised • Appropriate linking words/phrases are used to connect ideas • The summary is written using mostly own words • Very few errors in vocabulary and grammar
3–4	• Includes 3–4 content points • Only some content in the summary is relevant to the task	3–4	• Content points in the summary are partially organised • Appropriate linking words/phrases are sometimes used to connect ideas • The summary is written using some own words and some words taken from the original text • Some errors in vocabulary and grammar, but the content of the summary can be understood
1–2	• Includes 1–2 content points • Very little content in the summary is relevant to the task	1–2	• Content points in the summary are poorly organised • Linking words/phrases are rarely used or used incorrectly • The summary is written mostly using words taken from the original text • Frequent errors in vocabulary and grammar
0	• No content in the summary is relevant to the task OR • No attempt at the summary task	0	• Very inaccurate language is used OR • No attempt at the summary task

Exercises 5 and 6

Mark	Content (maximum 8 marks)	Mark	Language (maximum 8 marks)
7–8	**Relevance** • Question is answered fully • Style and register are appropriate for the text type • Excellent understanding of purpose and audience **Development of ideas (detail)** • Content is very well developed • Ideas are communicated clearly and effectively	7–8	**Range and complexity** • Wide range of vocabulary • Wide range of simple and complex structures **Accuracy** • Easy to understand • Errors are in less common vocabulary and complex structures **Organisation** • Ideas are organised effectively in a logical order • Wide range of linking words
5–6	**Relevance** • Question is answered fully • Style and register are mostly appropriate for the text type • Good understanding of purpose and audience **Development of ideas** • Content is developed	5–6	**Range and complexity** • Range of common vocabulary. Some less common vocabulary • Range of simple structures. Some complex structures **Accuracy** • Mostly easy to understand • Errors are mostly in less common vocabulary and complex structures **Organisation** • Ideas are well organised • Range of linking words
3–4	**Relevance** • Most of the question is answered • Style and register are quite appropriate for the text type most of the time • Some understanding of purpose and audience **Development of ideas** • Some development of content, but with some gaps or repetition • Sometimes unclear	3–4	**Range and complexity** • Mainly common vocabulary • Mainly simple structures **Accuracy** • Sometimes difficult to understand • Some errors in common vocabulary and simple structures **Organisation** • Reasonably well organised • Some linking words. Not always used well
1–2	**Relevance** • Only some of the question is answered • Style and register are inappropriate for the text type • Limited understanding of purpose and audience **Development of ideas** • Missing content, irrelevance and/or repetition • Often unclear	1–2	**Range and complexity** • Limited vocabulary • Limited structures **Accuracy** • Difficult to understand • Errors in common vocabulary and simple structures **Organisation** • Poor organisation. Few linking words
0	No marks can be given	0	No marks can be given

Speaking

Give a mark out of 10 for each category (structure, vocabulary, development and fluency), and then add these marks to give an overall total out of 30.

Mark	Structure	Vocabulary	Development and fluency
9–10	Uses a range of structures with accuracy and confidence	Uses a range of vocabulary to communicate sophisticated ideas with precision	Can hold a long conversation Can expand and develop the topic with original ideas Pronunciation is clear
7–8	Uses a range of structures with accuracy and confidence, but there are errors when using complex sentences	Uses enough vocabulary to communicate well	Can hold a conversation Responds relevantly with original ideas Pronunciation is generally clear
5–6	Uses simple structures with very few errors	Communicates simple ideas, not always successfully	Responds to questions and prompts, but sometimes needs help to continue with the conversation Pronunciation is understandable
3–4	Uses very simple, limited structures with errors. Communication is difficult	Limited vocabulary makes it difficult to communicate simple ideas, there is repetition and/or searching for words	Responses are brief with pauses Conversation is difficult Pronunciation is not always understandable
1–2	Rarely achieves communication	Cannot communicate simple ideas	Very brief responses Pronunciation difficult to understand
0	No response	No response	No response

Disclaimer: Please note that these mark schemes have not been produced by Cambridge Assessment International Education. The grade descriptors are based on Cambridge's descriptors but have been written by the authors of this resource. If you wish to see the official grade criteria for Cambridge IGCSE English as a Second Language, please visit the Cambridge Assessment International Education website.

Marking learners' work

Reading and Writing paper		
Exercises	**Answers which gain marks:**	**Answers which lose marks:**
Exercise 1	• short answers lifted from the original text • alternative answers which have the same meaning as the answer in the text	• poorly spelt answers where the meaning is not clear
Exercise 2	• clearly written letters	• more than one answer per question • a letter written over the initial answer which makes it difficult to decipher
Exercise 3	• ideas lifted from the text that are clearly different from one another • ideas written under the correct heading on a separate line	• ideas that are too similar (only 1 mark can be awarded for two similar ideas) • correct answers written under the wrong heading • paraphrased answers which change the meaning of the original idea in the text • answers that are misspelt which means the meaning is not clear
Exercise 4	• relevant ideas which focus on the aspect required (e.g. challenges, difficulties, advantages) • ideas (content points) which are clearly different from one another • ideas which are paraphrased from the original text as much as possible • ideas which are clearly organised and written as complex sentences with appropriate linking words • answers with a range of vocabulary (e.g. struggle, a daunting challenge, overcome) • answers with minimal errors	• ideas which don't match the aspect required (e.g. disadvantages instead of advantages) • irrelevant details which don't contain any correct ideas (content points) • ideas which use the same words/phrases as per original text • ideas which are written as short sentences with no linking words • answers which only contain a very limited range of very easy words (e.g. good, bad, do, don't like) • answers which are difficult to understand because of a lot of errors (e.g. grammar, spelling)
Exercise 5	• the email is informal • the email contains all the points from the question • all the information in the email is clearly organised into paragraphs and it is easy for the reader to understand • the ideas are well developed and easy to follow • ideas are linked using appropriate linking words • there is a range of vocabulary (e.g. phrasal verbs – get on with, set off and fixed phrases – I was in two minds) and grammatical structures (e.g. I've never done anything like it, I shouldn't have gone there) appropriate for an email • minimal errors	• the email uses the wrong register and a tone which would have a negative effect on the reader • some of the points from the question are omitted or the email goes off the topic • the information is not well organised, the writer jumps from one idea to another which makes it very difficult for the reader to understand, there are no paragraphs • the answers are very brief with no development • the sentences are very short with no linking words • the range of vocabulary and grammatical structures is very limited • answers which are difficult to understand because they contain a lot of errors (e.g. grammar, spelling) • answers which are too short

© Cambridge University Press 2018

Reading and Writing paper		
Exercises	**Answers which gain marks:**	**Answers which lose marks:**
Exercise 6	• the answer is in the correct style (i.e. article, report, review) and register (semi-formal to formal) • the answer deals with the topic from the question (e.g. a report about the school canteen and recommend what needs to be improved) and the reader would be fully informed • the answer contains well developed ideas (either from the prompts in the question or a learner's extra ideas) and gives examples of, and reasons for, these opinions • ideas are clearly organised into paragraphs (i.e. introduction of the topic/task, further information/ideas, conclusion/summary/recommendation) • ideas are introduced/logically linked with appropriate linking words (e.g. on the other hand, last but not least, as far as I'm concerned) • the answer contains a range of vocabulary and grammatical structures appropriate for the style and register • minimal errors	• the answer is in the wrong style, and register and uses a tone which would have a negative effect on the reader • the answer goes off the topic and the reader wouldn't be informed • the answer copies ideas from the prompts, these ideas are not developed and the whole answer contains no, or very little, extra information on the topic • ideas are poorly organised and there are no paragraphs • ideas are written as very short sentences with no linking words • the range of vocabulary and grammatical structures is very limited and inappropriate for the style and register • answers which are difficult to understand because they contain a lot of errors (e.g. grammar, spelling) • answers which are too short

Listening paper		
Exercises	**Answers which gain marks:**	**Answers which lose marks:**
Exercise 1	• short answers within the word limit, lifted from the recording • alternative answers which have the same meaning as the words in the recording (e.g. teamwork/working together)	• answers which are over the word limit • misspelt answers which make the meaning unclear • alternative answers which change the meaning of the answer in the text • correct answers written together with the distracting detail from the recording
Exercise 2 and 5	• one or two-word answers lifted from the recording • answers which fit the gap grammatically (e.g. singular/plural nouns, correct word forms – nouns/adjectives/verbs) • alternative answers which have the same meaning as the words in the recording (e.g. coach/trainer)	• answers that are over the word limit • answers which don't fit the gap grammatically • misspelt answers which make the meaning unclear • alternative answers which change the meaning of the answer in the text • correct answers written together with the distracting detail from the recording • answers which contain words/phrases/ideas already printed before/after the gap
Exercise 3		• the same letter used twice even if one of these answers is correct
Exercise 4		• answers where more than one box is ticked even if one of these answers is correct

Speaking paper		
Parts	**Answers which gain marks:**	**Answers which lose marks:**
Part D	• answers are well-developed and include examples of, reasons for, or comparisons of something, with the idea/opinion in the bullet point • the examiner asks extra questions to develop the topic further and the candidate can respond appropriately to this change in the conversation • delivery with clear pronunciation, rising and falling intonation, where appropriate, and at a natural speed so that the listener can understand • answers with a range of vocabulary and grammatical structures • minimal errors which result in a fluent and interesting conversation	• answers are very brief • answers are widely spaced and the examiner has to ask a lot of questions in order to maintain the conversation • delivery with poor pronunciation, flat/uninterested intonation and at an extremely slow or very fast speed so that the listener finds it very difficult to understand • very limited range of vocabulary and grammatical structures • frequent errors which mean the listener often doesn't understand and the conversation may break down

Tick sheets (self-assessment for learners)

The following tick sheets will help learners think about what is expected of them in the exam and to look more critically at their own performance.

Reading and listening tests		
Have you done the following? Put a tick in the appropriate box. HAVE YOU …	**Yes**	**No**
done what the instructions told you to do (e.g. use each letter only once)?		
written the answer on the line/in the space provided, under the correct heading, etc.?		
lifted the answer from the text/recording?		
written an answer that is within the word limit?		
provided a clear answer (e.g. crossed out the wrong answer to make sure your final choice is clear)?		
spelt your answer correctly?		
provided a grammatically correct answer?		
checked your answers after you finished doing the exercise/test?		

Writing test		
Have you done the following? Put a tick in the appropriate box. HAVE YOU …	**Yes**	**No**
answered all the points from the question?		
used the correct style (i.e. email, report, review, article) and register (i.e. informal, semi-formal)?		
developed your answers/ideas (e.g. given an example, explained the reason, agreed/disagreed with an idea)?		
used paragraphs?		
included a good beginning and end to your piece of writing?		
used complex sentences, where appropriate, and linking words/phrases?		
used a range of vocabulary and grammatical structures?		
used a capital letter to start a new sentence and a full stop or question mark to finish the sentence?		
spelt your words as correctly as possible?		
written a piece of writing of the right length?		
checked for mistakes and corrected as many as you could (e.g. tenses, missing/wrong prepositions)?		

 © Cambridge University Press 2018

Speaking test		
Have you done the following? Put a tick in the appropriate box. **HAVE YOU …**	Yes	No
talked about all five prompts on the topic card?		
given examples of your ideas/opinions?		
given reasons for your opinions?		
made some comparisons (e.g. you and your friends, now and in the past)?		
agreed/disagreed with the ideas on the topic card?		
given complex answers with appropriate linking words/phrases?		
made sure you sounded clear and interested in the topic?		
used a range of grammatical structures (e.g. tenses, conditionals, relative clauses)?		
used a range of vocabulary (e.g. descriptive adjectives and verbs, phrasal verbs, fixed expressions)?		
thought about the correct way of saying things in English to reduce the number of errors you make?		

Advice for learners

Before the exam

- familiarise yourself with the format of each part of the test
- learn about some useful exam techniques which will help you answer each part of the text more successfully
- do practice tests to see which parts you are good at and which parts you need to focus on more
- time yourself to see how much time you take to complete each part of the test
- look at your own mistakes and analyse them
- set yourself realistic targets

During the exam

- try to relax
- when you open the exam paper, first look through the whole test quickly to see what you have to do
- set yourself a time limit for each part of the exam to make sure you have enough time to complete each part
- try to use all the exam techniques you learnt in your lessons
- always spend a minute or two planning your answer in the writing part of the exam (e.g. what ideas to include, how many paragraphs, what information to include in each paragraph) before you start writing
- if you don't know an answer, guess – never leave any blank spaces
- if you change your answer, cross out the wrong answer to make it clear which answer is your final choice
- if you have enough time, check your answers

Practice Test 1

Reading and Writing

Exercise 1

Read the article about a woman called Li Daniels, who is a chef, and then answer the following questions.

LI DANIELS – COOKERY COMPETITION WINNER

Li Daniels grew up in the Malaysian city of Malacca, eating food influenced by Malay, Chinese, Indian and other food cultures. When she moved to Liverpool in the UK to study economics, she found things tough. Everything seemed so different, but the hardest thing to get used to was the food. 'I missed Malaysian food so much,' says Li. And she had no idea how to cook. Malaysians usually learn from their mothers, but Li's mother had always banned her from the kitchen. So, Li taught herself. She made mistakes at first, but soon grew to love cooking.

Li arrived in the UK ten years ago. She is now married to Chris Daniels, a businessman, and they have a three-year old son. They live in Liverpool, though their intention is to move to London in the next few months. 'It'd be more convenient for me,' says Li.

Besides cooking family meals, Li enjoys organising dinner parties for friends. About a year ago, someone suggested Li should try *The Big Taste*, a cookery competition on television. 'It was Gina, a colleague from the bank I'd recently joined,' says Li. 'I'd moved there from an insurance company.' Li had never dreamed of entering a cookery competition, let alone winning one and becoming a full-time chef. 'It's incredible how my life's changed because of what Gina said,' says Li. 'I'm even opening my own cafe later this year.'

Li entered *The Big Taste* with 50 other hopefuls. She survived ten weeks of challenges, from creating a tasty packed lunch to preparing a five-course meal for a special celebration, before reaching the final. 'Cooking for a top hotel was my personal highlight,' says Li.

It was an emotional experience for Li. 'I was really excited at first, but when the final became a possibility, I got very nervous.' In the last round, however, she was calm and cooked a wonderful seafood dish to win the contest. 'It was extraordinary,' said one of the judges.

Li won over viewers from the very first episode. They loved her warm character, and while many probably knew little about Malaysian cooking, they adored her creative approach. Her success brought her lots of attention from industry experts. Soon after her win, a publisher invited her to write a cookery book, and simply titled *Cooking with Li*, it has just been published. Li was also asked to supply some well-known restaurants with recipes and she says that will happen by the end of the year.

Li bases her recipes on traditional south-east Asian dishes, but she experiments with them. Her sister and a few friends help her with ideas, and her husband tastes every recipe she comes up with. 'His opinion's important to me,' she says.

Before she started work on the cookery book, Li had concerns about whether she was a good enough writer. Those doubts soon disappeared, but there was one unfortunate consequence of working on lots of new dishes: she put on over five kilos in weight. 'It's one of the dangers of the job,' she says.

© Cambridge University Press 2018

Li is now busier than ever. Besides looking after her family and promoting her book, she gives demonstrations at food festivals and in restaurants. She is also preparing to launch a cookery school next year, and she is in discussions with a television company and hopes to start filming a documentary series about spices in the coming few months.

'The Big Taste changed my life,' says Li. 'I do so many different things now. I couldn't survive without my diary. I depend on it more than my cooker or my kitchen knives!'

1 How did Li learn to cook?

.... [1]

2 Where was Li working when she entered the cookery competition?

.... [1]

3 Which part of the competition did Li enjoy most?

.... [1]

4 How did Li feel during the competition final?

.... [1]

5 What made Li so popular with television audiences? Give **two** details.

....

.... [2]

6 Who else always tries out Li's new dishes?

.... [1]

7 What problem did Li have when she was writing her book?

.... [1]

8 What does Li think is her most important possession nowadays?

.... [1]

9 What plans does Li have for the future? Give **four** details.

....

....

....

.... [4]

[Total: 13]

Exercise 2

Read extracts from a magazine article in which four people (**A–D**) talk about the night before an important day in their working lives. Then answer Question **10 (a)–(j)**.

THE NIGHT BEFORE A BIG DAY

A   Actor, Harry Mcneill

Actors are always in the theatre the night before the first public performance of a play. We spend time running through our lines, but everyone involved in the production is there doing the final preparations for the next day. My mind plays tricks on me when the pressure is on. I've been acting for nearly 10 years, and I'm better than I used to be, but I still get visions of myself in front of a big audience not being able to remember anything I'm supposed to say or do. Some actors find a space where they can be alone and rest, but that doesn't suit me. I get anxious if I'm not doing something. Acting is mentally and physically exhausting, so it helps to keep fit, but I also get through a considerable quantity of sandwiches and pizza – far more than is good for me. When I eventually get home and into bed, I usually experience very little difficulty in falling asleep.

B   Astronaut, Simone Katz

I will soon be on my third space mission. On both previous occasions, I carried out repairs to the Space Station and was only there for a few days. This time, however, I'll be there for three months, doing research, spacewalks and lots of everyday tasks. I can't wait and I'll feel exactly the same on the eve of departure. I'm currently going through a training programme to get my physical fitness and skills to the levels required. By the night before take-off, I'll have adopted all the eating, sleeping and exercise patterns that we have to follow in space; there won't be any great party. On that last night, however, I'll telephone my parents and sister to say goodbye. Judging by my previous experiences, the conversations are unlikely to be relaxed; everyone knows things can happen in space, however carefully you prepare. I will also try to ensure that I get a few valuable hours to myself. It's rarely available when you're with your crew in the Space Station.

C   Professional cyclist, Matthew Jones

In the races I take part in, we can cover 3000 kilometres in under three weeks. We cycle huge distances every day and we have to be extremely fit and well-prepared. In the evening after a day's racing, I always have a large meal before I start again the following day. Professional cyclists like me are usually very slim, but you'd be surprised how much we eat; the food gives us energy. In the meantime, my bike receives any necessary maintenance. Without my back-up team, I wouldn't be able to compete. At some point in the evening, I chat to my wife and son online. I'm away from home so much and for me it's vital to have that regular contact with them. I go to bed at nine o'clock and I usually listen to some music – nothing too challenging – to take my mind off the race. It's better for me to start the next stage feeling fresh than to worry about it overnight, and music helps me relax and sleep.

© Cambridge University Press 2018

D Surgeon, Monica Alvarez

Although I've been a surgeon for over ten years, I still have trouble sleeping well the night before a big operation. This used to upset me, but I've come to see it as normal. Operations can be long and exhausting and I may do three or four in a day. Twelve-hour working days are not uncommon, but surgeons learn how to deal with all this. In fact, I'd say that all the surgeons I know have strong characters and they are proud of the responsibilities they are given. In the evening before a major operation, I avoid doing anything very energetic. I usually sit down to a good dinner with my husband and children and we catch up on each others' days. My children don't always understand why I always ask them about what they've been doing at school and with their friends, and what they are going to do tomorrow, but like any parent, I want to know these things.

10 **The questions below are about the people (A–D) who talk about the night before an important day in their working lives.**

For each question write the correct letter A, B, C or D on the line.

Which person ...

  a accepts that they may not sleep well? .... [1]

  b looks forward to future events? .... [1]

  c imagines how things could go wrong for them? .... [1]

  d tries to avoid thinking about the following day? .... [1]

  e feels the need to spend some time on their own? .... [1]

  f prefers to stay busy? .... [1]

  g explains what they rely on other people for? .... [1]

  h thinks they eat too much? .... [1]

  i suggests that other people in the same profession have similar feelings? .... [1]

  j finds it difficult to talk to family members? .... [1]

[Total: 10]

Exercise 3

Read the article about a dinosaur expert called James Bruce, and then complete the notes on the following page.

THE DINOSAUR EXPERT

James Bruce is one of the world's leading palaeontologists. In other words, he is a dinosaur expert who studies fossils, the remains of animal bones that are millions of years old. He hasn't always been interested in dinosaurs. 'I had other hobbies when I was a kid,' he says.

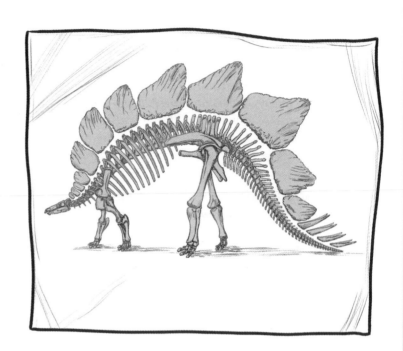

James' interest was sparked at 14 when he saw a dinosaur movie at the cinema. 'I loved the special effects and the idea that such amazing animals had been on earth millions of years ago,' he says. 'Then I got obsessed with theories of what caused the dinosaurs to disappear. That still fascinates me and I wish I had time to study it now.' Twenty-five years after that cinema trip, James spends a lot of time travelling around the world looking for dinosaur fossils. 'I'm so lucky to be doing that,' he admits.

His experience as a teenager is one reason why he is unwilling to criticise dinosaur movies. He understands that they are meant to entertain, and the fact that the dinosaurs in them move much faster than was actually the case 100 million years ago doesn't concern him. 'The ones you see in films are also a lot more intelligent than they could possibly have been,' he says. 'But if the films get people interested in dinosaurs by telling a good story, that's a good thing.'

James has spent some of the last three years advising makers of TV documentaries on the subject of dinosaurs. 'That's great fun,' he says. He checks that the animals reconstructed for the documentaries are as close as possible to what scientists know about dinosaurs. 'In the movies, dinosaurs are shown as darker and less colourful than they were in reality,' he says. 'That's to make them look scary. I make sure the dinosaur figures in the documentaries are colourful.'

However, James admits there's much that is still unknown about dinosaurs. 'We have very little idea about how they interacted with each other – you can't work it out just from studying bones,' he says. Also, there are various theories about what sounds dinosaurs might have made, but the evidence is limited. 'I'm very keen to investigate both of those issues,' James says.

James' main job is at a university where he is professor of palaeontology. 'Some of my colleagues just want to do research and don't much like teaching but it gives me great satisfaction,' James says. What he is less keen on is the time and energy he has to devote to raising funds to pay for the new research projects that he loves coming up with.

One project that he worked on was part of a wider international programme, which established that modern-day birds are directly related to dinosaurs. It was this discovery that led James and other palaeontologists to conclude that many species of dinosaur were covered with feathers. 'All the dinosaurs we see when we go to the cinema are featherless and that's not what most were like,' he says.

Palaeontology is a fast-moving field with new discoveries being made all the time. Fossils are regularly found, and previously unknown species are identified. Experts are continuing to investigate issues of great importance. 'We still don't know much about how dinosaurs originally developed,' says James. 'It's something I'd be very keen to do some work on if the opportunity arose.'

You are going to give a talk about the dinosaur expert to your class at school. Prepare some notes to use as the basis for your talk.

Make short notes under each heading.

11 The aspects of his work that James particularly likes

Example: travelling around the world looking for dinosaur fossils

- ....
- ....
- .... [3]

12 How movie dinosaurs are different from the real dinosaurs

- ....
- ....
- .... [3]

13 Questions about dinosaurs that James would like to do more research on

- ....
- ....
- .... [3]

[Total: 9]

Exercise 4

14   Read the following article about children and music.

Write a summary about how children can benefit from music.

Your summary should be about 100 words long (and no more than 120 words long). You should use your own words as far as possible.

You will receive up to 8 marks for the content of your summary and up to 8 marks for the style and accuracy of your language.

IS MUSIC ACTUALLY GOOD FOR YOU?

In the early 1990s, some people thought that if you played recordings of music by the classical composer Mozart to babies, their brain power would increase. Studies since then have shown that this so-called 'Mozart effect' does not exist. However, there is plenty of evidence that active and regular involvement in music can be very good for children.

In one experiment carried out in London, psychologists studied the effect that singing along to songs by the pop band Blur had on a group

of children, and there have been similar studies with different types of music. In each case, the researchers reached the conclusion that the activity makes children happier. What's more, as a result, they perform difficult tasks better. Most of us, of course, know from personal experience that music can have this impact. We also know that music-making often happens in groups of various kinds and we recognise music as something that is shared with others. Researchers have found that this aspect of music-making can help pre-teens develop valuable social skills.

Psychologists have also looked at more specific issues. They have discovered, for example, that babies and infants who are encouraged to clap and sing along to a variety of songs tend to learn to speak faster than babies who don't have this experience. Other studies have shown that children who receive music education of some kind – at home with parents, in nursery or at school – are often particularly good at learning other languages. Other researchers have observed that when children learn about musical rhythms, patterns and timing, their ability to deal with numbers improves. In other words, there is often a connection between having some music training and being good at maths.

It's not very surprising that music should have an impact. 'Physical exercise and training over time changes a person's body and makes them better at doing things like sport,' says psychologist Dr Evelina Hutz. 'It's similar with hearing and learning about music, though probably more in terms of the brain.'

Musical education is not only intellectual, however. It can also be physical. Research indicates that children who learn to dance and play musical instruments tend to develop good physical coordination. Those who are trained to dance, for example, are more likely than others to be able to move in a smooth and efficient way.

It has also been found that musical training improves children's memory and their ability to concentrate. These qualities are clearly very valuable. 'The more you think about it,' says Dr Hutz, 'the more obvious it is that music should be a central part of education.' One country where music is given priority in schools is Finland and, interestingly, on international tests, Finnish children regularly achieve higher scores in various subjects than most other countries in the world.

One quality that can contribute hugely to an individual's success in almost any field is self-confidence, and it seems clear that children who have some form of musical education have greater self-confidence. 'Research studies provide plenty of good evidence of this,' Dr Hutz says.

Music education is often treated as an optional, extra subject, offered only if children have time and special talent. The evidence, however, suggests that it should be provided regularly to all children.

....

....

....

....

....

....

....

....

....

....

....

....

....

....

....

.... [Total: 16]

© Cambridge University Press 2018

Exercise 5

15 You recently helped to organise a special celebration at your school.

Write an email to a friend explaining what happened. In your email, you should:

- explain what the celebration was for

- describe how you helped to organise the celebration

- say why you think it's important for schools to organise celebrations.

The pictures above may give you some ideas, and you can also use ideas of your own.

The email should be between 150 and 200 words long.

You will receive up to 8 marks for the content of your email, and up to 8 marks for the language used.

....

....

....

....

....

....

....

....

....

....

....

....

....

....

....

....

....

....

....

....

....

.... [Total: 16]

Exercise 6

16 A local newspaper is planning to publish reviews of books that are good for young people to read. You decide to write a review of a book that you and some of your friends have read. In your review, explain what the book is about and say why you think other young people should read it.

Here are two comments from your friends who have read the book:

> *The book has some very interesting characters.*

> *The book isn't always easy to read.*

Write a review for the newspaper.

The comments above may give you some ideas, and you can also use some ideas of your own.

Your review should be between 150 and 200 words long.

You will receive up to 8 marks for the content of your review, and up to 8 marks for the language used.

....

....

....

....

....

....

....

....

....

....

....

....

....

....

....

....

....

....

....

....

.... [Total: 16]

© Cambridge University Press 2018

BLANK PAGE

Practice Test 1

Listening

Exercise 1

🔊 **CD1 audio tracks 02, 03, 04, 05**

You will hear four short recordings. Answer each question on the line provided. Write no more than **three** words for each answer.

You will hear each recording twice.

1   **a**   What new thing does the girl have in her room?

.... [1]

    b   What is the girl going to do next to improve her room?

.... [1]

2   **a**   What was the man most worried about before the race?

.... [1]

    b   What does the man think is the reason for his good result?

.... [1]

3   **a**   What does the boy think is special about the songs by his favourite singer?

.... [1]

    b   Why was the boy disappointed by the concert given by his favourite singer?

.... [1]

4   **a**   What does the woman say was difficult about organising the birthday party?

.... [1]

    b   What pleased her grandad most about the party?

.... [1]

[Total: 8]

Audio for the listening exercises is on the CDs and online at cambridge.org/education/igcse-esl-tests.

Exercise 2

🔊 **CD1 audio track 06**

5 You will hear a talk given by a man who visited the Baja Desert in Mexico. Listen to the talk and complete the sentences below. Write **one** or **two** words only in each gap.

You will hear the talk twice.

Tom's holiday in the Baja Desert

Tom's first holiday activity was ....

He decided to spend his second day on the coast ....

He had to buy .... before starting his trip to the desert.

Being in the desert reminded Tom of a ....

He was amazed by the .... of some of the desert plants known as cacti.

In the desert Tom learnt about one type of plant that was used to produce a .... in the past.

Tom was disappointed that he didn't see a .... there.

Tom was impressed by some .... he saw at the end of his trip.

[Total: 8]

Audio for the listening exercises is on the CDs and online at cambridge.org/education/igcse-esl-tests.

Exercise 3

🔊 **CD1 audio track 07**

6   You will hear six students talking about experiments they did in science lessons. For each of Speakers 1 to 6, choose from the list, **A** to **G**, which opinion each speaker expresses. Write the letter in the appropriate box. Use each letter only once. There is one extra letter which you do not need to use.

You will hear the recordings twice.

Speaker 1 ☐

Speaker 2 ☐

Speaker 3 ☐

Speaker 4 ☐

Speaker 5 ☐

Speaker 6 ☐

A   I wish I'd listened to advice from my friends.

B   Working with others proved more fun than expected.

C   I found the work very challenging.

D   I was surprised by the good results.

E   It took a long time to prepare everything.

F   It has changed my attitude to science.

G   The mistakes I made weren't too serious.

[Total: 6]

Audio for the listening exercises is on the CDs and online at cambridge.org/education/igcse-esl-tests.

Please turn over for Question 7.

© Cambridge University Press 2018

Exercise 4

🔊 **CD1 audio track 08**

7 You will hear an interview with a woman called Jo Baylis, who is a radio presenter. Listen to the interview and look at the questions.

For each question, choose the correct answer, **A, B** or **C**, and put a tick (✓) in the appropriate box.

You will hear the interview twice.

a Jo decided to become a radio presenter because

   A she was excited about an experience her father had. ☐

   B she believed that she had the right personality for it. ☐

   C she loved a particular radio programme. ☐ [1]

b What does Jo say about her first experience of being on the radio?

   A She had too little time to prepare before her first show. ☐

   B She was disappointed by the lack of training offered. ☐

   C She was too nervous to perform well. ☐ [1]

c Jo prefers to present programmes which focus on

   A discussing different topics. ☐

   B introducing new music. ☐

   C reviewing films and TV programmes. ☐ [1]

d What does Jo say about having to get up early in the morning to present her show?

    A Jo needs time to get herself into the right mood. ☐

    B Jo has overcome her initial problems with it. ☐

    C Jo regrets the effect it has on her social life. ☐ [1]

e What does Jo say about the comments she gets from her listeners?

    A Jo tries to respond to all the points people make. ☐

    B Jo wishes people would try to be more positive. ☐

    C Jo is surprised by the range of opinions people have. ☐ [1]

f What does Jo say is the most difficult aspect of her job?

    A Coming up with new ideas for each programme. ☐

    B Having to maintain a high level of concentration. ☐

    C Having to do so many different things. ☐ [1]

g According to Jo when she presents a programme, she

    A has to think carefully about the impression she wants to give. ☐

    B sometimes feels uncomfortable about not seeing her audience. ☐

    C imagines she is talking to a group of her friends. ☐ [1]

h Jo doubts that she will ever become a TV presenter because

    A she is afraid she might not be successful at it. ☐

    B she wants to improve her skills in her current job. ☐

    C she thinks it is unlikely she would be offered work. ☐ [1]

[Total: 8]

Audio for the listening exercises is on the CDs and online at cambridge.org/education/igcse-esl-tests.

Exercise 5

🔊 **CD1 audio track 09**

8 a   You will hear a science teacher called Mr Hamilton giving a talk about asteroids, which are rocky worlds revolving around the Sun. Listen to the talk and complete the notes in part **(a)**. Write **one** or **two** words only.

You will hear the talk twice.

Asteroids

Asteroids are most commonly known as ....

The majority of asteroids are .... in shape.

The teacher was surprised to find that some asteroids have ....

The most common type of asteroid is .... in colour.

The teacher doesn't like the fact that there are asteroids named after ....

[5]

Audio for the listening exercises is on the CDs and online at cambridge.org/education/igcse-esl-tests.

🔊 **CD1 audio track 10**

8 b Now listen to a conversation between two students about asteroids and complete the sentences in part **(b)**. Write **one** or **two** words, or a number, in each gap. You will hear the conversation twice.

Student research on asteroids

Parts of an asteroid become a threat to Earth when they measure about .... or more across.

.... were used to find asteroids from 1800 onwards.

One spacecraft sent to an asteroid obtained some .... which was important for research.

Both students are surprised that .... could possibly be mined on asteroids in the future.

As a priority, elements contained inside asteroids could be used to produce ....

[5]

[Total: 10]

Audio for the listening exercises is on the CDs and online at cambridge.org/education/igcse-esl-tests.

BLANK PAGE

Practice Test 2

Reading and Writing

Exercise 1

Read the article about a young artist called Kieron Williamson, and then answer the following questions.

KIERON WILLIAMSON – TEENAGE ARTIST

Like many other 14-year-old boys, Kieron Williamson spends as much time as he can playing football with his friends. Off the pitch, however, he has less in common with his peers. Since the age of six, when some of his drawings and paintings were first exhibited, he has been called a 'mini genius,' and his art has made him a millionaire.

After being given a sketchbook and some colouring pencils during a family holiday, Kieron, then five, set to work. 'I'd never drawn anything before,' he says, 'but I fell in love with it straight away.' When they saw his first efforts, Kieron's parents, Michelle and Keith, quickly realised he had an unusual ability, and it wasn't long before a local gallery invited him to contribute to an exhibition – something he was very happy to do. Michelle and Keith were amazed when they found out that the gallery had sold all of his work within a few days.

The popularity of Kieron's art has grown remarkably ever since. 'It's crazy,' his father admits. But despite all the money he has earned, Kieron doesn't spend much. He has little interest in computer games, unlike most of his friends, and although he's very keen on cycling, he's satisfied with the rather plain bike that he's had for some years. What he likes most is to work on his art, although he does take pleasure in listening to music while painting. Recently, he has included more people in his pictures, but the majority have always been of countryside scenes.

Kieron paints quickly and produces hundreds of paintings a year. They all get bought up by collectors from around the world. How does he manage it? He realises he has talent, but he believes the key is his determination. He puts pressure on himself to maintain standards, although this sometimes brings frustration. 'I can spend all day trying to make a picture work without success,' he says. He's worked out what to do about it, however. He leaves the picture for a day. Then, when he eventually comes back to it, a solution often comes.

When Kieron's artistic career took off, his parents gave up their own jobs so they could look after the sales of his art. They also wanted to deal with the public attention that his art was attracting. In order to protect their privacy, Michelle and Keith eventually concluded the family had to move to a quieter location. They all miss their old village, but they are happy in their new house and have made friends in the local community.

Michelle and Keith also took Kieron and his sister Billie-Jo out of school and started to home-educate them. Both siblings wish they still had the chance to carry on joking around with their friends, as they used to do in class, but both respond well to the individual attention they now get. Kieron is particularly grateful for the time he can now devote to art.

Kieron thinks he is very lucky to have had the chance to explore his creativity, and he is keen to help other teenage painters explore theirs. He thinks they should learn from each other in art groups, and he is looking into ways of setting up something that would help in this respect. He also recommends that teenagers paint outside. He believes that he himself has benefited hugely from doing this.

The house where he now lives has fields and woods all around, and it is a great place for observing animals. This is one of his favourite pastimes, in fact, and he even has a plan to buy and keep a few cows nearby.

1   How old was Kieron when his art began to attract public attention?

.... [1]

2   How did Kieron's parents feel when people started to buy Kieron's paintings?

.... [1]

3   What is the main topic of Kieron's paintings?

.... [1]

4   What does Kieron think is the most important quality he has?

.... [1]

5   What does Kieron do when he can't make progress with a painting?

.... [1]

6   Why did Kieron's family decide to leave their old home?

.... [1]

7   What does Kieron miss most about his old school?

.... [1]

8   What advice does Kieron offer young artists? Give **two** details.

....

.... [2]

9   What hobbies apart from art does Kieron have? Give **four** details.

....

....

....

.... [4]

[Total: 13]

Exercise 2

Read extracts from a magazine article in which four students (**A–D**) write about working as volunteers on archaeological projects. Then answer Question **10 (a)–(j)**.

VOLUNTEERS ON ARCHAEOLOGICAL PROJECTS

A   Abdi Hassan

Last summer, my friend Sara asked me if I'd be interested in working as a volunteer with her on an archaeological project in Italy. She'd wanted to do something like this for years, but was nervous about going there alone. We ended up having such an interesting time that I'm thinking about doing it again next year. All the volunteers were based in the same student residence, and we helped archaeologists investigate the remains of some 3000-year-old buildings. We had to dig up bits of ancient tiles, pottery and bones, and clean them carefully using special knives and brushes. The archaeologists in charge were great at explaining things and keeping everyone happy. It was so different from my normal life. It was too hot to do anything in the afternoons, so we got up at 4 a.m. while it was cool, and worked through the morning. Then we did more in the evenings. It was really tough. I eventually adapted to things, but it took me a while.

B   Angela Choo

Earlier this year, I spent a month as a volunteer on an archaeological project in Peru. If I'd known how brilliant it was going to be, I'd have arranged to spend another month there, but that wasn't possible in the end, unfortunately. Along with other volunteers, I helped archaeologists who were responsible for investigating and maintaining some remains from the ancient Inca civilisation. We mostly had to clear away trees and other plants that had grown on the sites. We did it with saws and huge knives called machetes. Using these might look quite straightforward, but it wasn't, as I soon realised. Living and working high in the mountains was tough. There's less oxygen up there, so it can be hard to breathe, which was a shock initially, but I loved my time there. One day, I actually found a piece of Inca jewellery. The archaeologists kept it to examine more closely, but finding it was such a thrill. I'd never imagined anything like that would ever happen.

C Raul Valencia

I'm an archaeology student and I've worked as a volunteer on several different projects. The most recent was on Orkney Island off the north of Scotland, where there are some important remains of 5000-year-old Stone Age settlements. Working on a Stone Age site was a dream of mine and actually getting to do it was great, especially because some well-known and respected archaeologists run the project. As I have some experience, I didn't just do the basic work; they asked me to take measurements of Stone Age walls, and record objects that people had discovered, which was quite complicated sometimes. There are lots of really interesting ancient objects buried under the ground there. It can get very windy, wet and cold on Orkney, and you could never describe the hostel where the volunteers stay as comfortable, but it's a beautiful, fascinating place which is definitely worth visiting.

D Kirstin Michaels

I spent two weeks working at the site of some ancient Roman ruins in a very remote location in Romania. The living quarters were simple but clean, and I can't imagine anyone not falling in love with the place. It was the first time I'd ever travelled to a different country by myself, and there had been a few questions on my mind, like: What if the people are unfriendly? What if the food isn't to my taste? I needn't have worried. Everything was wonderful, even on days when all I did was use a spade and a fork to dig large holes so the researchers could see what lay under the surface. I knew they might come across some valuable historical evidence down there. I'm not particularly suited to that kind of heavy work, but I think I did a good job. In fact, one of the archaeologists thanked me and said I'd managed to do more than most volunteers manage in twice the time.

10 **The questions below are about the students (A–D) who worked as volunteers on archaeological projects.**

For each question write the correct letter A, B, C or D on the line.

Which person ...

a is pleased to have been able to fulfil an ambition? .... [1]

b mentions finding the daily schedule hard to get used to? .... [1]

c regrets not staying on the project longer? .... [1]

d feels proud of a physical achievement? .... [1]

e mentions the difficulty of working with certain tools? .... [1]

f feels inspired to do more archaeological work in future? .... [1]

g admits to being anxious before joining the project? .... [1]

h mentions the excitement of making an unexpected discovery? .... [1]

i suggests that some people might dislike the accommodation at the site? .... [1]

j praises the skills of the project leaders? .... [1]

[Total: 10]

Exercise 3

Read the article about space debris, rubbish that has been left by humans in space, and then complete the notes on the following page.

MAN-MADE SPACE DEBRIS

In August 2016, engineers at the European Space Agency (ESA) realised that something was wrong with their most important observation satellite. They quickly worked out that the satellite, orbiting 35 000 kilometres from the earth, had been hit by a tiny piece of debris. 'It could have been something like a piece of soap,' says one engineer. 'That might seem strange, but all sorts of things have been left in space and they travel at very high speeds – over ten kilometres per second.' Fortunately, the engineers were able to carry out repairs. Satellites and spacecraft require millions of dollars of investment, however, and the incident was a reminder that one day a very expensive piece of technology could be destroyed by space litter.

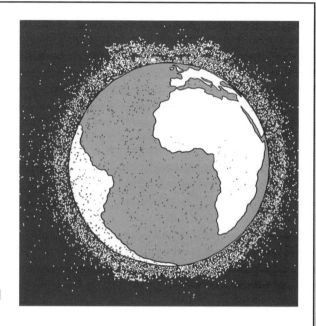

Sputnik, the first ever man-made satellite was launched in 1957, and since then, over 5000 satellites have been sent into space. However, only about 1200 of them are currently working; the rest are no longer used and just orbit the earth like large pieces of junk. It's not so surprising that these 'dead satellites,' and even large parts of broken spacecraft, are a form of space pollution. But there are thought to be about 150 million man-made objects larger than one millimetre in size, and many of them are things that most people wouldn't imagine were in space. Bits of paint and old batteries have been reported, and while they may not seem significant, they can be very dangerous.

'There is so much space debris,' says one ESA engineer, 'that some sections of space may eventually become unusable.' Scientists at the ESA are currently working on plans for spacecraft which function as space garbage trucks; these would pick up rubbish and bring it back to earth. Projects like this are costly and difficult, however, and experts stress the need for international agreements about dealing with man-made objects in space.

'Satellites and other spacecraft are equipped with radars and cameras which detect large objects, so they can avoid them,' says the ESA engineer. 'But the systems can't always detect objects of a more limited scale – like a bit of unused fuel or even a tool lost by an astronaut during a space-walk. There's also the fact that, at some point, human life may be at risk. Don't forget that there are people working on the International Space Station and in other spacecraft, and their numbers are likely to grow.'

Unfortunately, the near future is likely to become even more complicated. Large companies are planning to launch several thousand new satellites into space in order to provide improved communications and internet access for all parts of the world. This makes the need to deal with space debris even more urgent. One possible solution relates to the design of satellites: when a satellite becomes out-of-date, it should automatically return to earth.

Dealing with smaller waste is, in some ways, more complicated. A research project in the USA is aiming to develop laser beams, which would push rubbish out of orbit. Another project in Japan is building a giant net that would collect small waste over a period of time. It would then be directed back to earth and its contents would burn up upon entering the Earth's atmosphere.

Some of the ideas being considered are difficult to imagine, but solutions for dealing with man-made space litter are clearly needed.

You are going to give a talk about space debris to your class at school. Prepare some notes to use as the basis for your talk.

Make short notes under each heading.

11 Examples of small pieces of space debris

Example: a piece of soap

- ....

- ....

- .... [3]

12 Problems that space debris could cause in the future

- ....

- ....

- .... [3]

13 Ideas for clearing up space debris

- ....

- ....

- .... [3]

[Total: 9]

Exercise 4

14 Read the following article written by an athletics coach about running the marathon.

Write a summary about the mental preparation people should do before they run a marathon.

Your summary should be about 100 words long (and no more than 120 words long). You should use your own words as far as possible.

You will receive up to 8 marks for the content of your summary and up to 8 marks for the style and accuracy of your language.

RUNNING THE MARATHON

Fifty years ago the marathon was a minority sport, but it started to change in the 1970s. Today, marathon races are huge events attracting thousands of runners of all types: world champions, keen amateurs, women as well as men, old and young, disabled people, and many who will only ever run one marathon.

It's not easy to run 42 kilometres, so why do so many people choose to do it? In my experience, it's often that they want to challenge themselves. When I help people with their training, I usually remind them that they have chosen this challenge, and my first piece of advice is to tell yourself you can do it. Although 42 kilometres is a long way, thousands manage it every year.

Of course, a lot of the preparation is about getting physically fit, and that is one reason why many people enter the marathon. You have to run several days a week over a number of months to be in the right shape. This is hard, and unless you are an experienced runner, you won't be able to do long distances immediately. It helps to work out short-term goals that you can achieve. This is actually a good approach for many challenges we have in life.

When you are training, there will be times when you struggle, with your legs hurting and being out of breath. It's a good idea to consider how you will deal with difficult situations in advance. You probably won't find the answers overnight, but you are sure to find some eventually. All runners experience pain; you can't avoid it, unfortunately. The trick is for you to work out how to block pain when it comes. This probably won't be easy, but different techniques can be used. You may have decided to enter the marathon in order to help a charity, as many people do. If so, when you're finding your training a challenge, focus on the money you will raise – it's a good thing to occupy your mind with.

When runners are exhausted while training, they tend to look down at the ground. This doesn't help, however. As I always say to the runners I train, make yourself look up and around you as you run. This will take away some of the anxiety and pressure. In a similar way, if you're training and you feel desperate to stop, think about the respect you will gain from others when they realise how far you can now run.

Because the marathon requires such a lot of physical preparation, it's very common for runners to get injured when they are training. This happens to professional athletes as well as people doing it for the first time. Some people get depressed when this happens, but my advice is always to take pride in all the running you've already done. This will give you fresh motivation.

I hope that I haven't made marathon training sound too unappealing. The fact is that it's a very tough challenge. On the other hand, as you're training, you should remember that it will be very good for your health. It's also true that you can have a wonderful time doing it. So, don't forget to enjoy yourself. If it just makes you feel miserable, there's no point doing it.

.... [Total: 16]

Exercise 5

15   You recently went on a class visit to a museum.

Write an email to a friend about the visit. In your email, you should:

- describe the museum that you went to

- explain what you liked about the museum

- say how the museum could attract more young people.

The pictures above may give you some ideas, and you can use ideas of your own.

The email should be between 150 and 200 words long.

You will receive up to 8 marks for the content of your email, and up to 8 marks for the language used.

....

....

....

....

....

....

....

....

....

....

....

....

....

....

....

....

....

....

....

....

.... [Total: 16]

Exercise 6

16 Your class has recently been studying different environmental problems. Your teacher has asked you to write a report about an environmental issue in your school. In your report, describe something about the school that you think is bad for the environment and suggest what could be done to improve the situation.

Here are two comments from other students in your class:

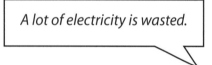

A lot of electricity is wasted.

Regular activities to pick up litter around the school would be good.

Write a report for your teacher.

The comments above may give you some ideas, and you can also use some ideas of your own.

Your report should be between 150 and 200 words long.

You will receive up to 8 marks for the content of your review, and up to 8 marks for the language used.

....

....

....

....

....

....

....

....

....

....

....

....

....

....

....

....

....

....

....

....

.... [Total: 16]

BLANK PAGE

Practice Test 2

Listening

Exercise 1

🔊 **CD1 audio tracks 11, 12, 13, 14**

You will hear four short recordings. Answer each question on the line provided. Write no more than **three** words for each answer.

You will hear each recording twice.

1 **a** What subject is the girl's online blog about?

.... [1]

   b What does the girl find most difficult about blogging?

.... [1]

2 **a** What did the boy paint for the art competition he entered?

.... [1]

   b How did the judges describe the painting the boy did?

.... [1]

3 **a** What did the boy learn about chocolate when he was at the factory?

.... [1]

   b What type of flavour did the boy have in his chocolate bar?

.... [1]

4 **a** What new clothes did the girl buy for herself?

.... [1]

   b What did the girl dislike about the shop?

.... [1]

[Total: 8]

Audio for the listening exercises is on the CDs and online at cambridge.org/education/igcse-esl-tests.

Exercise 2

🔊 **CD1 audio track 15**

5   You will hear a talk given by a man called Josh Collins, who helped organise a carnival in his town. Listen to the talk and complete the sentences below. Write **one** or **two** words only in each gap.

You will hear the talk twice.

Organising this year's carnival

The carnival took place in the month of ....

There was a .... in the park for people to enjoy.

People taking part in the carnival parade started at the ....

Josh thinks that the .... were the best part of the carnival this year.

It was suggested to people attending the carnival that they could come as

.... if they wanted.

.... food was introduced to the carnival this time.

On the day of the carnival, Josh was responsible for the ....

The final event of the carnival was ....

[Total: 8]

Audio for the listening exercises is on the CDs and online at cambridge.org/education/igcse-esl-tests.

Exercise 3

🔊 **CD1 audio track 16**

6   You will hear six people talking about their experiences of learning about history. For each of Speakers 1 to 6, choose from the list, **A** to **G**, which opinion each speaker expresses. Write the letter in the appropriate box. Use each letter only once. There is one extra letter which you do not need to use.

You will hear the recordings twice.

Speaker 1	☐	**A**	I had to make a lot of effort but it was worth it.
Speaker 2	☐	**B**	I appreciated how history helps us understand the present.
Speaker 3	☐	**C**	I realised I needed to study the subject in more detail.
Speaker 4	☐	**D**	It was difficult for me to imagine life in the past.
Speaker 5	☐	**E**	I found all the dates rather boring.
Speaker 6	☐	**F**	I understood how history is connected to other subjects.
		G	I found some explanations confusing.

[Total: 6]

Audio for the listening exercises is on the CDs and online at cambridge.org/education/igcse-esl-tests.

Please turn over for Question 7.

Exercise 4

🔊 **CD1 audio track 17**

7   You will hear an interview with a woman called Rachel Smith, who is a sailor. Listen to the interview and look at the questions.

For each question, choose the correct answer, **A, B** or **C**, and put a tick (✓) in the appropriate box.

You will hear the interview twice.

a   When Rachel first went to a sailing club, she

    A   was surprised by what she learnt from the talk.   ☐

    B   was embarrassed about making a mistake.   ☐

    C   had to pretend to enjoy the sailing experience.   ☐   [1]

b   What does Rachel say about the first time she was at sea for several days?

    A   She spent a lot of time on boring routine tasks.   ☐

    B   She worried about the crew's attitude to her.   ☐

    C   She was given a chance to take on big challenges.   ☐   [1]

c   According to Rachel, sailing in a small boat

    A   meant she put herself in some danger.   ☐

    B   taught her things that were useful later on.   ☐

    C   embarrassed her because it wasn't well-equipped.   ☐   [1]

d Rachel says that an ideal crew member would be someone who is

    A able to deal with difficult situations calmly. ☐

    B willing to do the necessary training with her. ☐

    C friendly and can see the funny side of things. ☐ [1]

e What did Rachel find most difficult about the first race she took part in?

    A the lack of time she had to get ready ☐

    B the quality of the opposition she faced ☐

    C the terrible weather conditions ☐ [1]

f Rachel says that at the beginning most of her competitors

    A said things that affected her confidence. ☐

    B found it hard to believe she was doing so well. ☐

    C were sometimes willing to give a limited amount of help. ☐ [1]

g When Rachel is on a long sailing trip she

    A is in constant contact with home. ☐

    B finds it difficult to spend time by herself. ☐

    C has so much to do there isn't time to feel sad. ☐ [1]

h Rachel thinks winning the race across the Atlantic was special because

    A she had been unable to get much rest. ☐

    B she wasn't concentrating at important moments. ☐

    C she had to use equipment that didn't work properly. ☐ [1]

[Total: 8]

Audio for the listening exercises is on the CDs and online at cambridge.org/education/igcse-esl-tests.

Exercise 5

🔊 **CD1 audio track 18**

8 a You will hear a man called Eddie Granger giving a talk about his visit to a place called the Butterfly Centre. Listen to the talk and complete the notes in part **(a)**. Write **one** or **two** words only.

You will hear the talk twice.

The Butterfly Centre

At the Butterfly Centre, it is difficult to keep the .... at an appropriate level.

One staff member, Eddie spoke to, was responsible for .... butterflies.

Eddie was surprised to see a lot of .... which are important in the life cycle of many types of butterfly.

Many people don't know how sensitive butterflies are to ....

When visiting the centre, Eddie benefited from the ....

[5]

Audio for the listening exercises is on the CDs and online at cambridge.org/education/igcse-esl-tests.

CD1 audio track 19

8 b Now listen to a conversation between two students about attracting butterflies to gardens and complete the sentences in part **(b)**. Write **one** or **two** words only in each gap.

You will hear the conversation twice.

Making a garden attractive to butterflies

The decline in butterfly numbers is mostly due to ....

It's not widely known that having some .... in a garden is necessary for butterflies.

The girl's grandmother says that .... make butterflies come to her garden.

Experts recommend that gardeners avoid ....

The boy hopes that he might see a butterfly called the ....

---

[5]

[Total: 10]

Audio for the listening exercises is on the CDs and online at cambridge.org/education/igcse-esl-tests.

BLANK PAGE

Practice Test 3

Reading and Writing

Exercise 1

Read the article about a trip to see wild gorillas in the Volcanoes National Park, in Rwanda in Africa, and then answer the following questions.

GORILLA TREKKING

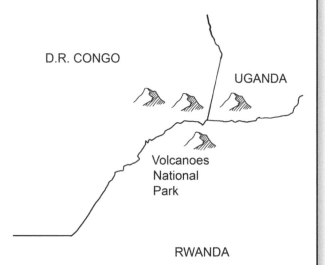

Earlier this year, while on a short holiday in Rwanda in Africa, I saw some wild mountain gorillas in their natural environment. Gorilla trekking – going on long, tough walks to see the animals – is a significant tourist activity in the Virunga Mountains, which extend across both Rwanda and Uganda. The treks offered in the Volcanoes National Park of Rwanda tend to be shorter than those in Uganda's National Park, which is why that option suited me.

Gorilla trekking is a year-round activity, though during the 'long rains' of April and May, conditions are very wet and hiking is at its toughest. The peak season for visitors in July and August is followed by a second rainy season from September to November. The fact is, however, that it can rain at any time, which is why visitors should always have waterproof clothes, and waterproof bags are also needed to protect camera equipment.

All treks have to be supervised by park rangers who guide visitors to one of several gorilla groups. The rule is there, above all, to protect the gorillas, but, also, most visitors wouldn't be able to do much without guides. Gorillas are good at hiding and the mountain slopes are challenging; the vegetation is so dense and rough that trekkers are advised to bring gardening gloves to protect their hands, and long-sleeved tops to stop their arms getting badly scratched.

All visitors must attend an introductory information session. If you miss this, you are not allowed to trek. You can be turned away for other reasons too, as was the case with one visitor I saw. This American woman had flu, which the gorillas have no natural resistance to. Each group of visitors goes in search of one particular gorilla family, called a troop, and the trek, including one hour with the troop, may take anything between three and nine hours.

My group hiked for over four hours through thick vegetation along steep, slippery paths. I appreciated my strong walking boots, a must for anyone trekking in the area. I was also glad to have packed a good pair of binoculars, following a tip on the park website, as there were all sorts of amazing birds and other wildlife to observe. Our guides told us there were 19 gorilla troops in the park, with 10–30 individuals in each one. There are thought to be about 500 wild gorillas in the region, almost double the number estimated in 1981, when conservation efforts began to have an effect. Mountain gorillas live at altitudes between 2500 and 4000 metres, and to help them deal with the cold temperatures, they have longer fur than gorillas living at lower altitudes elsewhere in Africa. They also tend to be larger than the other species of gorilla.

When we finally found our gorilla troop, it consisted of two older males, several mothers, younger males and females and at least two babies. Some were sleeping, some were eating leaves and some of the younger ones just seemed to want to play with each other. We kept about seven metres away from them, but they clearly knew we were there. At one point, one of the larger males started to come in our direction. They're big, powerful animals and I must admit to feeling nervous, but I did what we'd been told: keep still, which is always sensible when you're near them. They aren't aggressive but it's best to avoid eye contact when they approach, just in case. After a minute or two, the male lost interest and we were left to enjoy the privilege of observing the extraordinary creatures close-up.

1   Why did the writer choose to see the gorillas in Rwanda rather than in Uganda?

.... [1]

2   Which are the busiest months of the year for gorilla trekking?

.... [1]

3   What is the main reason that visitors are supervised in the Volcanoes National Park?

.... [1]

4   Why was someone stopped from going on a trek when the writer visited?

.... [1]

5   How long are visitors allowed to spend near the gorillas?

.... [1]

6   In what ways are mountain gorillas physically different from lowland gorillas? Give **two** details.

....

.... [2]

7   What should visitors do if a gorilla moves towards them? Give **two** details.

....

.... [2]

8   What things are visitors recommended to take with them? Give **four** details.

....

....

....

.... [4]

[Total: 13]

Exercise 2

Read extracts from a magazine article in which four students (**A–D**) write about studying drama at university. Then answer Question **9 (a)–(j)**.

DRAMA STUDIES

A   Isabel Monteiro

When I tell people I'm studying drama at university, they often say things like, 'It's all about acting, so how can you study it?', or 'Sounds like three years of having fun'. The fact is, though, my course is seriously hard work. We work on our acting, singing, directing and stage management skills, but we also do research, essays and exams, like students on other courses. We work a lot in teams, and as most jobs in theatre, film-making and television involve working with other people, this makes sense. In fact, team-working skills are useful for all sorts of jobs unrelated to drama. Because we spend so much time together – not only studying, but living and socialising too – we become very close friends. Other students notice this, and I've heard them describe us as a little strange and hard to understand. This may have something to do with us all being rather loud and outgoing, but you'd expect that in people attracted to performing.

B   Femi Mensah

I originally went to university to study literature, but I soon realised that a course which included physical activity, performance and creativity, as well as reading and writing, would suit me better. So, I switched to drama studies, and I've never regretted it. This year we did a brilliant project which involved forming a small-scale theatre company and writing, producing and performing a play. This kind of project requires lots of teamwork, but you're allowed lots of freedom to choose how you do things. This does mean you have to be well-organised and strict about managing your time, and I've learned a lot from working like this. My teachers have told me, and I know they're right, that I'm not a naturally talented performer, so I may not end up working in the theatre. The truth is, however, that graduates from my course have become teachers, marketing professionals, even police officers, and I'm sure they use skills they developed on this course.

C   Natalya Vasiliev

One thing I hadn't realised before I started my drama course was how much theatre and film work relies on a willingness to cooperate. You might be putting on a play in a wonderful theatre with very advanced lighting and sound equipment, as I'm fortunate to be able to do in my university, but you can't avoid working with people who have very different attitudes and approaches. You have to learn to deal with it. As far as I'm concerned, that's a key part of being a drama student. In fact, I'll probably never work in an environment where no-one complains to me and everyone always gets on well, whatever field of work I eventually find myself in. Playwriting is one of the many skills I've been able to develop on my course, and I'd actually like to write plays for a living. If this is not possible, I'll have to look into other jobs I could do.

D Takashi Kimura

I'm in the final year of my drama course and I'm thinking about what I should do next. I'd like to be a theatre actor, though I would be able to do backstage jobs like managing the lighting or the sound because of the different areas we've covered on the course. Finding work is often very challenging for young actors. One of the benefits of studying drama here is that we meet people from the worlds of theatre, film and television, and I've even done work experience at one of the top theatres in the city. I've tried to stay in touch with people I've met because they might be able to help me in future. Everyone says you need to be strong to survive as an actor, and I feel I've become tougher through the projects and performances we've done. Our teachers always point out when you've done something wrong or below standard, and you learn to cope with feedback like that.

9   The questions below are about the students (**A–D**) who study drama at university.

For each question write the correct letter **A**, **B**, **C** or **D** on the line.

Which student mentions …

a   the wide range of different careers that drama students go into?   .... [1]

b   the value of developing a network of contacts?   .... [1]

c   the appeal of high-quality facilities?   .... [1]

d   a characteristic that many drama students share?   .... [1]

e   satisfaction with the balance between academic and practical work?   .... [1]

f   a difficult aspect of doing lots of group work?   .... [1]

g   a common misunderstanding about drama studies?   .... [1]

h   the importance of being able to handle criticism?   .... [1]

i   the value of self-discipline?   .... [1]

j   the relationships that drama students develop?   .... [1]

[Total: 10]

Exercise 3

Read the article about a man called Greg Preston, who teaches people how to surf, and then complete the notes on the following page.

GREG PRESTON – THE MAN WITH THE DREAM JOB?

For many people it sounds like a dream job. Twenty-eight-year-old Greg Preston teaches people how to surf on Seven Mile Beach in south-east Australia from September to April. Then, from May to August, he goes overseas to teach surfing; in the last five years he's been to Indonesia, Mexico, France, Sri Lanka and South Africa.

'My work gives me the chance to travel, which is something I love,' he says. 'I'm very lucky really because I love my job too. I'm passionate about surfing. In fact, I don't think you can teach it if you're not.'

Greg has been surfing for ten years. He got into it as a student living in Sydney. 'I grew up in Canberra, the capital of Australia,' he says. 'Canberra's about 150 kilometres inland from the coast, and I'd only been to the seaside once before I moved to Sydney, so I find the idea of living and working by the sea just fantastic.'

Greg admits that not everything about the job is ideal. 'You earn very little money teaching people how to surf,' he says. 'The other thing is that you have to keep an eye on the learners all the time, which I'm very happy to do by the way, but it means you don't have much time to surf yourself. That's frustrating sometimes. But no job's perfect, I suppose.'

Three years after he started surfing, Greg reached an advanced level and trained to become a qualified instructor. 'You don't have to be qualified to be able to teach surfing,' Greg says. 'But it's essential to be very aware of safety, and the instructor courses are helpful for that.'

As in many sports, there are risks involved in surfing. Something that Greg never looks forward to is telling students that they can't go into the water. 'The sea is too dangerous sometimes,' he says, 'but people get very disappointed when they can't have lessons. I don't know why they find it so hard to accept. You just have to explain the situation to them. They get their money back if there are no classes, of course. But I don't think you can do the job properly unless you're a good communicator.'

Greg says that he gets asked lots of questions about surfing and about his job. His students come from many different backgrounds. His current class includes two college students, a Japanese tourist, a farmer, two builders, an artist and an engineer. But the same questions are asked again and again, like 'What's the biggest wave you've ever ridden?' and 'Is part of your job fixing the surfboards when they get damaged?', to which Greg replies 'Yes, and it puts me in a bad mood'. Other common questions are 'Do you ever see sharks?' and 'Do you have to be very fit to teach surfing?' The answer to the last question is 'absolutely,' Greg says. He doesn't mind answering the questions, even though they can be repetitive. In fact, the opportunity to meet a wide variety of people appeals to him greatly, and although he only sees his students for a few lessons, he builds up a relationship with them. 'There's nothing more satisfying,' he says, 'than seeing a student managing to ride a wave.'

© Cambridge University Press 2018

You are going to give a talk about the work of a surf instructor to your class at school. Prepare some notes to use as the basis for your talk.

Make short notes under each heading.

10 What Greg likes about being a surf instructor

Example: the chance to travel

- ....
- ....
- .... [3]

11 What Greg dislikes about being a surf instructor

- ....
- ....
- .... [3]

12 What Greg believes a surf instructor needs to be

- ....
- ....
- .... [3]

[Total: 9]

Exercise 4

13 Read the following article about flying cars.

Write a summary about the possible advantages and disadvantages of flying cars.

Your summary should be about 100 words long (and no more than 120 words long). You should use your own words as far as possible.

You will receive up to 8 marks for the content of your summary and up to 8 marks for the style and accuracy of your language.

FLYING CARS

The idea of private vehicles which drivers can use to travel through the air and on the ground has been around for about a century, but until recently no-one has been able to construct a flying car that works. There have been major technological advances in recent years, however, and a number of large companies are now developing flying cars. The models created so far tend to look more like mini-airplanes than traditional cars, but is it likely that some kind of flying car will soon be available to buy?

It's not hard to understand why the idea is popular. They would be able to move much faster through the air than normal cars on the road. Also, while cars on the ground have to drive through complicated road systems, especially in urban areas, flying cars could go straight from A to B. The appeal of flying cars seems obvious and if it's now possible to make them, isn't it likely that we will see many of them in the skies above us before long?

Many people have their doubts. According to transport expert Alex Kirwan, 'while the technology of flying cars is now very advanced, safety is still a big issue. When a normal car has a breakdown, the driver can usually stop by the side of the road and get out. It's unclear what would happen if something went wrong with a vehicle flying through the air.' Kirwan also thinks that bad weather conditions are a serious concern when it comes to flying cars. 'I recently drove through a major storm,' he says, 'and I had to go very slowly because of the wind and rain. Several hundred metres up in the air the wind is much stronger.'

Fans of the idea of flying cars point out that they could be used to avoid traffic jams. 'If you think about what many cities are like these days, this does make flying cars sound great,' says Professor Farah Ghorbani. 'But setting up an air traffic control system for them would be a huge challenge. We'll definitely need one if there are going to be thousands of vehicles buzzing around above our cities and towns.' Professor Ghorbani thinks there's another problem that won't be easy to solve. 'No-one knows what skills and permits people will need to operate flying cars,' she says. 'For driving on the ground, we have lessons, tests and licences. What are we going to do about driving in the sky?'

Engineer Jin Pak, who has worked on a Korean flying car project, points out that 'flying cars don't require road systems which are expensive to build and maintain.' On the other hand, he admits that lots of places to take off from and land on will be needed. Jin also agrees that the cost will prevent most people from owning them for many years. 'A flying car for one or two people will be several times more expensive than a standard car,' he says. 'There's absolutely no doubt about that.'

So, it seems unlikely that flying cars will be a common sight any time soon. Having said that, not very long ago, few people imagined they would ever own a single small device that could do everything a smartphone is capable of.

© Cambridge University Press 2018

[Total: 16]

Exercise 5

14 One of your teachers recently gave you some advice about a problem that you had.

Write an email to a friend explaining what happened. In your email, you should:

- describe the problem that you had

- explain the advice that the teacher gave you

- say whether the advice has been useful and why.

The pictures above may give you some ideas, and you can also use ideas of your own.

The email should be between 150 and 200 words long.

You will receive up to 8 marks for the content of your email, and up to 8 marks for the language used.

© Cambridge University Press 2018

.... [Total: 16]

Exercise 6

15 An international student magazine wants to publish some articles about different festivals around the world. You decide to write an article about a festival in your country that you think young people in other countries would find interesting. In your article, describe what happens in the festival and explain why you think the festival is important for people in your country.

Here are two comments from other students in your class:

> *It brings people together.*

> *It's very different from what people do the rest of the year.*

Write the article for the magazine.

The comments above may give you some ideas, and you can also use some ideas of your own.

Your article should be between 150 and 200 words long.

You will receive up to 8 marks for the content of your article, and up to 8 marks for the language used.

© Cambridge University Press 2018

[Total: 16]

BLANK PAGE

Practice Test 3

Listening

Exercise 1

🔊 **CD2 audio tracks 02, 03, 04, 05**

You will hear four short recordings. Answer each question on the line provided. Write no more than **three** words for each answer.

You will hear each recording twice.

1 **a** Where was the fashion show held?

.... [1]

    b Why does the girl think the fashion show was successful?

.... [1]

2 **a** Where does the cartoon film begin?

.... [1]

    b Why does the man think the cartoon will be popular?

.... [1]

3 **a** What impressed the girl most about the football match?

.... [1]

    b How does the boy describe the captain of the team?

.... [1]

4 **a** What does the air museum need money for the most?

.... [1]

    b What type of aircraft is new to the air museum?

.... [1]

[Total: 8]

Audio for the listening exercises is on the CDs and online at cambridge.org/education/igcse-esl-tests.

Exercise 2

🔊 **CD2 audio track 06**

5   You will hear a talk given by a young man called Ray Cole, who cycled through seven countries in Central America. Listen to the talk and complete the sentences below. Write **one** or **two** words only in each gap.

You will hear the talk twice.

Cycling in Central America

When planning the trip, Ray was worried about his ....

He wasn't interested in .... during the cycling trip.

Ray said that a .... was the most impressive landscape he saw.

Ray found the .... was the biggest problem for him.

He enjoyed staying in .... during his trip.

When cycling, he found that eating .... was very helpful.

During the last part of his trip, Ray was disappointed that his .... stopped working.

After the trip, he shared his experiences in a ....

[Total: 8]

Audio for the listening exercises is on the CDs and online at cambridge.org/education/igcse-esl-tests.

Exercise 3

🔊 **CD2 audio track 07**

6 You will hear six people talking about meals they have had. For each of Speakers 1 to 6, choose from the list, **A** to **G**, which opinion each speaker expresses. Write the letter in the appropriate box. Use each letter only once. There is one extra letter which you do not need to use.

You will hear the recordings twice.

Speaker 1	☐	**A**	The variety of food was great.
Speaker 2	☐	**B**	It wasn't planned very carefully.
Speaker 3	☐	**C**	The location made the occasion special.
Speaker 4	☐	**D**	It was an opportunity to meet new people.
Speaker 5	☐	**E**	The atmosphere changed quite quickly.
Speaker 6	☐	**F**	The number of people caused problems.
		G	It was more fun than I expected.

[Total: 6]

Audio for the listening exercises is on the CDs and online at cambridge.org/education/igcse-esl-tests.

Please turn over for Question 7.

Exercise 4

🔊 **CD2 audio track 08**

7 You will hear an interview with a woman called Isabelle Navarro, who manages rock bands. Listen to the interview and look at the questions.

For each question, choose the correct answer, **A, B** or **C**, and put a tick (✓) in the appropriate box.

You will hear the interview twice.

a Isabelle Navarro prefers to work with people who have

    A shown some ability to organise themselves.

    B already managed to achieve something locally.

    C a strong belief in their ability to do well.   [1]

b Isabelle says that she decided to manage her first band because

    A she realised she could never be a singer.

    B she was inspired by a book about famous managers.

    C she thought it would be quite easy to do.   [1]

c How did Isabelle feel when her first band had a hit record?

    A She was unsure that she had played an important role.

    B She was worried the success would not be repeated.

    C She was surprised by the attention she received.   [1]

d   Isabelle says her advice to new rock bands would be to

    A   try to record their first album as soon as they can. ☐

    B   discuss with other musicians what they should do. ☐

    C   have the courage to ignore the latest fashion in music. ☐   [1]

e   What does she say about her relationship with the band the Big Cats?

    A   It was sometimes necessary to annoy the band members. ☐

    B   It lasted much longer than she expected it to. ☐

    C   It took a long time for both sides to trust one another. ☐   [1]

f   Isabelle usually manages only soft rock bands because

    A   she has a reputation for success with such musicians. ☐

    B   she has loved that type of music all her life. ☐

    C   she has limited knowledge of other types of music. ☐   [1]

g   Isabelle believes that a successful manager of a rock band needs to

    A   be willing to work very long hours. ☐

    B   react to constant problems seriously. ☐

    C   be able to take on many completely different roles. ☐   [1]

h   How does Isabelle think that the music business has changed in recent years?

    A   Bands ask for their fans' opinions about what they should do. ☐

    B   Bands expect to become successful very quickly. ☐

    C   Bands are less likely to work with a manager. ☐   [1]

[Total: 8]

Audio for the listening exercises is on the CDs and online at cambridge.org/education/igcse-esl-tests.

Exercise 5

🔊 **CD2 audio track 09**

8 a You will hear a talk by an oceanographer, a scientist who studies the sea. Listen to the talk and complete the notes in part **(a)**. Write **one** or **two** words only.

You will hear the talk twice.

The work of oceanographer, Oliver Connors

Oliver started his career researching .... , although it wasn't his main interest.

His most exciting project involved investigating a ....

On his latest mission, his team are using a .... to explore the ocean floor.

He was surprised to have discovered some .... on this mission.

When he thinks about the future, his greatest worry is ....

[5]

Audio for the listening exercises is on the CDs and online at cambridge.org/education/igcse-esl-tests.

🔊 **CD2 audio track 10**

8 b Now listen to a conversation between two students about exploring and protecting the oceans and complete the sentences in part **(b)**. Write **one** or **two** words, or a number, in each gap.

You will hear the conversation twice.

Exploring and protecting the oceans

The students both think that .... are the most beautiful marine creatures.

The Mariana Trench, located in the Pacific Ocean, is now thought to be .... kilometres deep.

The students didn't know about the .... in the Mariana Trench.

The students think .... is the science that can benefit most from the work of oceanographers.

The girl would like to participate in work to protect ....

[5]

[Total: 10]

BLANK PAGE

Practice Test 4

Reading and Writing

Exercise 1

Read the article in which a journalist, called Gavin Stevens, describes how he climbed Aconcagua, a mountain in South America, and then answer the following questions.

CLIMBING ACONCAGUA

I had always dreamed of climbing to the top of a really high mountain. 'How about Aconcagua in Argentina?' a friend suggested. 'It's nearly 7000 metres high and you can get to the top without rock-climbing skills.' I did some research and then booked my place on a guided climb in January this year.

My climbing group consisted of eight people, all from different countries, and was led by three local guides. We had set off from the entrance of Aconcagua Provincial Park and hiked for three days across grassland, desert and rocky hills to get to Base Camp. At one point, a sandstorm delayed us for five hours, but the walking built up our strength.

At 4300 metres above sea level, Aconcagua Base Camp, as I'd seen in photos online, is a strange-looking collection of colourful tents, toilet and shower facilities, a helicopter pad and even a volleyball court. There was also a plastic palm tree, which seemed completely out of place to me.

We stayed there for four days to get used to the altitude. With low oxygen levels, it's hard to sleep and you feel breathless and dizzy. We rested and chatted to other climbers. One Korean had climbed Kilimanjaro, the highest mountain in Africa. 'Aconcagua's more challenging for climbers,' he said. 'It's 1000 metres higher.' He showed me photos he'd taken of both mountains. 'I don't think Aconcagua's quite as beautiful as Kilimanjaro, but the weather here's definitely more extreme,' he added.

Before we moved up to Camp 1, one of our team was forced to drop out because of a chest infection. Another climbing-mate, Susana, said: 'It could get really bad if he carries on.' She's a doctor, and I felt fortunate to be climbing with her.

We stayed two nights at Camp 1. At that altitude (5000 metres), it's essential to drink lots of water, but it's too heavy to be carrying a lot. The guides solve this problem by collecting snow to melt for tea, and I was happy to give them a hand with this while others in the group checked the weather forecasts.

On the two nights we spent at Camp 2 (5550 metres), the temperature dropped below minus 30°C and the wind was incredibly strong. To stop it destroying our tents, we built walls of rocks around them, but sleep was almost impossible. After the first night there, a Brazilian woman in our team decided she couldn't go on. She was suffering from severe exhaustion, so a guide accompanied her back to Base Camp.

On the night we spent at Camp 3 (6000 metres), the wind dropped a little, but it snowed. Our guides' reaction surprised me. 'The final stage has lots of small loose rocks,' one explained. 'The path's easier to walk on if there's snow.' On the last day of the climb, we set off at 5 a.m. Our progress was very slow. At 6300 metres, one of the climbers had no feeling in her feet or hands. The guides said it was too risky for her to continue, and one of them would take her down. Hearing this, another climber who was having serious problems breathing said he would go with them.

That left four of us with one guide. We eventually reached the top after eleven days of sleeplessness, breathlessness and pain. We completed the last stage in nine hours. It was tougher than anything I'd ever experienced, but, for one hour, we stood on the highest place on earth outside the Himalayas. We took photos, ate something, and then it was time to descend. I had achieved my ambition.

 © Cambridge University Press 2018

1 What made the hike to the Base Camp slower than usual?

.... [1]

2 What was the writer surprised to see at the Base Camp?

.... [1]

3 Why is Aconcagua harder to climb than Mount Kilimanjaro in Africa? Give **two** details.

....

.... [2]

4 Why was Susana a good person to have in the group?

.... [1]

5 How did the writer help the guides at Camp 1?

.... [1]

6 How did the climbers protect their tents from the wind?

.... [1]

7 Why were the guides pleased when it snowed?

.... [1]

8 How long did the final section of the climb take?

.... [1]

9 What reasons did four of the writer's group have for giving up before they reached the top of Aconcagua mountain? Give **four** details.

....

....

....

.... [4]

[Total: 13]

Exercise 2

Read the reviews of four computer games (**A–D**). Then answer Question **10 (a)–(j)**.

REVIEWS OF COMPUTER GAMES

A 'Planet Kree'

When Arsenio Vroom lands his damaged spacecraft on the planet Kree, he finds himself in the middle of a battle for control of the distant planet. This reminds me of science fiction games I used to play 15 or 20 years ago, and so do the soundtrack and even the types of tasks you have to deal with as a player. I must admit that I loved all this about it. Generally, younger gamers in particular are likely to enjoy the cartoon-like art and the jokey, often weird communication between the characters, but there may not be as much to keep the interest of a more mature generation of players – apart from the occasional individual like me. The game starts with us following Arsenio, but we soon meet lots of other fantasy characters. In fact, there are so many that you forget who is who, what they have done and what they are trying to do. Apart from this, however, the game is excellent.

B 'Motorbike Marvels'

Motorbike fans will love this game, and I can't see why it shouldn't appeal to people who are too young to have ever sat on a motorbike. The bikes look fantastic as they speed around the racetracks, and the game designers have definitely managed to recreate the thrilling atmosphere and the amazing range of colour and movement you get at races. You can play solo or with others online, and you can choose your competitions, riders and bikes. These range from beautiful classic models from 50 or 60 years ago to super-advanced modern machines. It's a pity the difficulty levels are often much too high in the races, and there's nothing you can do to change this. I lost count of the number of times my riders crashed. On the other hand, I loved playing the role of racing team manager. Lots of detailed information is provided about the bikes and each rider – personality, riding style, career records, and so on – and it all seems very realistic.

C 'Settlers'

In 'Settlers', players control a group of travellers who settle and establish a new community in an unnamed country. They give the characters traditional roles and tasks. One, for example, becomes a builder who constructs homes and other buildings for the community; another organises entertainment. Some tasks seem much more demanding than others. Basically, it's an update on 'Villagers', which came out about ten years ago. In my view, 'Settlers' doesn't have enough new features to make it really satisfying, but it has its strong points. The characters are all likeable, perhaps unrealistically so, and unlike many games of this type, it is remarkably free of technical problems. If your preference is for fast-moving, all-action games, then 'Settlers' is unlikely to be your first choice. I got much more enjoyment out of playing it with a couple of friends than I did playing it on my own, and I imagine this would be true for most people.

D 'Tracks'

Some music games are well-made and popular. 'Guitar Hero' and 'Rock Band' are two that come to mind, but many don't really work. A lot of them do exactly the same things, and then a few others are too complex for ordinary gamers to cope with. 'Tracks' is different. The idea is that a group of friends gather in a recording studio to make a record. Players control the musicians and studio engineers, and eventually create an album of whatever musical style or quality they like. It's a long and tricky process, which I first thought might be rather boring, but actually I found it to be completely the opposite. I loved trying out different sounds and instruments, from classical violins and organs to the latest electronic devices. Creative people often have unusual personalities, and the musicians in this game are no exception. In fact, some are so extreme that they are unbelievable – it would be better if they weren't like that. But I still loved the game.

10 The questions below are about the reviews of computer games (**A–D**).

For each question write the correct letter **A, B, C** or **D** on the line.

Which reviewer ...

a thinks the game is too similar to previous versions of it? .... [1]

b finds the game surprisingly exciting? .... [1]

c suggests that the game wouldn't suit all ages? .... [1]

d praises the game for being reliable? .... [1]

e thinks the story in the game is too complicated? .... [1]

f says that some of the challenges in the game are unfair? .... [1]

g suggests it is better to play the game with other people? .... [1]

h wishes the characters were more natural? .... [1]

i appreciates the old-fashioned style of the game? .... [1]

j is impressed by the visual effects in the game? .... [1]

[Total: 10]

Exercise 3

Read the article about a professional table tennis player called Arjun Chandran, and then complete the notes on the following page.

THE PROFESSIONAL TABLE TENNIS PLAYER

Thirty-two-year-old Arjun Chandran is one of the best table tennis players in India. Three years ago he was among the top 200 players in the world, and he has competed in many countries including the USA, Japan and China. His experiences in China made a big impression on him. 'Chinese players win most of the medals at the major international competitions,' he said. 'When you go to China, though, it doesn't seem that surprising. Far more people play table tennis there than anywhere else in the world.'

Arjun enjoys visiting China. 'I like the people and the culture,' he says, 'and playing there has helped me develop as a player.' He says their table tennis facilities are excellent, and is convinced that they help to explain the high quality of Chinese players.

Arjun has been a professional player for 12 years, and he believes players are now much fitter than when he started out. He has had to work hard to keep up with his rivals, but it has been worth it.

A small increase in the size of the balls is another fairly recent development. Table tennis as played by professionals is extremely fast, and the aim was to make it easier for people watching to see what was happening. Also, the ball now moves through the air a little more slowly than before.

But Arjun thinks further changes are needed to make the sport more spectator-friendly. At present, in international competitions, a single ball is used throughout a match, unless it gets damaged and needs replacing. Arjun thinks it would be better to have several balls available for players to use. 'The game would flow better,' he says. 'In fact, there are too many delays during matches – taking turns to serve every two points, having some water, and so on. These things irritate spectators so there should be fewer breaks, even if some players don't like that.'

It has been suggested that the net should be higher, but Arjun believes this would only help certain types of players. 'We now have more variety of playing styles than in the past,' he says. 'I'm quite aggressive, but others are defensive or technical – and I think that makes things interesting for people watching.' What he would like, however, is stricter rules about the rubber covers on the players' bats. There are many different ones and they affect the way players hit the ball. Arjun thinks this confuses members of the public.

Two years ago, Arjun set up a children's table tennis academy in India, having seen similar schools in China. 'Kids there start playing table tennis very young – at five or six. All those medals that the Chinese win are partly a result of this. Indian players usually don't start playing until they're 15. It makes a big difference.' Arjun has also seen very advanced training methods in China. He believes they are a key factor in the Chinese success story, and he wants young Indian players in his school to benefit from them.

'One of the great advances in my time as a player has been much better analysis of opponents before matches,' says Arjun. 'I think I can teach young players to do that.' Arjun has not yet retired from international competitions, but his future is clear: to do everything he can to help young Indian table tennis players.

You are going to give a talk about Arjun Chandran and his views on table tennis to your class at school. Prepare some notes to use as the basis for your talk.

Make short notes under each heading.

11 How professional table tennis has changed during Arjun's career

Example: players are (now much) fitter

• ....

• ....

• ....

• .... [4]

12 Reasons why Chinese table tennis players are the best in the world

• ....

• ....

• .... [3]

13 Arjun's ideas for making table tennis more popular with spectators in the future

• ....

• .... [2]

[Total: 9]

© Cambridge University Press 2018

Exercise 4

13 Read the following article written by a wildlife photographer called Marina.

Write a summary about the things that Marina says people should do to take good wildlife photographs.

Your summary should be about 100 words long (and no more than 120 words long). You should use your own words as far as possible.

You will receive up to 8 marks for the content of your summary and up to 8 marks for the style and accuracy of your language.

WILDLIFE PHOTOGRAPHY

Growing numbers of people are taking up wildlife photography as a hobby. I'm a professional photographer, but I also run courses for young people who want to learn how to take wildlife photos. There are a number of things I always tell them they need to do, and these recommendations are also useful for anyone keen to learn how to do wildlife photography.

I always advise my students to start with a project on a particular subject. Many of them can't decide exactly what to do at first, but it definitely helps them develop their skills so that they can take more effective photos. I also encourage my students to look for wildlife at dawn and dusk. That's when photographers are most likely to get interesting images. I spend a lot of time reminding my students to think carefully about the light. It often takes new photographers time to really understand how important this is, but it's one of the basic things you have to learn to be a good photographer. I always insist that my students check the weather forecast too. It's something that I have learned to do from my own personal experience of taking photographs of a wide range of wildlife in different parts of the world.

When I first started taking photos, I was given a lot of advice and practical help by an older photographer I had met called Annie Martens. Before setting out to photograph a particular species of wildlife, she always used to do some research into the animal's behaviour. It might seem quite an obvious thing, and it's something I make sure I do now. You would be surprised, however, at how many photographers actually know very little about the animals they are taking images of, and it affects the quality of their work. Something else that I learned from Annie Martens was to take photos from the same eye level as the animal. This is not always easy to do. In fact, I have been in many situations where I have felt very uncomfortable doing it. The images I ended up with, however, are among the best I have ever taken.

Another thing that the best photographers do is to think about the background of the photograph. Students understand the importance of this, but it's often difficult to get it right. Also, I always get students to try to tell a story in a photo. As an example of what I mean, a few years ago one student of mine took a series of photographs of wild birds surrounded by buildings. At first glance, the images didn't seem to be particularly interesting, but the more you looked at them, the more they made you think about how the birds had adapted to an urban environment.

 © Cambridge University Press 2018

Taking good wildlife photos is never straightforward, and students often feel disappointed with the results of their work at first. I always insist that they keep trying. It may seem obvious to you, but I think it's worth saying. One thing that can often make a difference is to experiment with different camera settings. They can be confusing at first, but most people are eventually able to use them well enough.

....

....

....

....

....

....

....

....

....

....

....

....

....

....

....

....

....

....

....

.... [Total: 16]

© Cambridge University Press 2018

Exercise 5

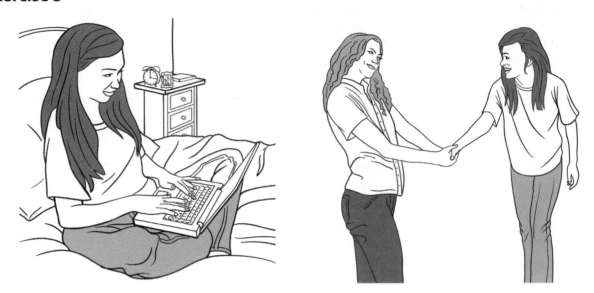

15 You recently found the email address of an old friend who you haven't seen or spoken to for two years.

Write an email to your old friend. In your email, you should:

- ask for some information about your friend's life in the last two years

- explain what your life has been like

- suggest that you and your friend meet up and what you can do.

The pictures above may give you some ideas, and you can also use ideas of your own.

The email should be between 150 and 200 words long.

You will receive up to 8 marks for the content of your email, and up to 8 marks for the language used.

.... [Total: 16]

Exercise 6

16 You recently went with some friends to a concert in the area where you live. You decide to write a review of the concert for your school magazine.

Here are two comments made by friends who went to the concert with you:

> *Some of the concert was very different from what I expected.*

> *Lots of people in the crowd got really excited.*

Write the review for the magazine.

The comments above may give you some ideas, and you can also use some ideas of your own.

Your review should be between 150 and 200 words long.

You will receive up to 8 marks for the content of your review, and up to 8 marks for the language used.

  © Cambridge University Press 2018

[Total: 16]

BLANK PAGE

Practice Test 4

Listening

Exercise 1

🔊 **CD2 audio tracks 11, 12, 13, 14**

You will hear four short recordings. Answer each question on the line provided. Write no more than **three** words for each answer.

You will hear each recording twice.

1 **a** Who has done something special at the school this year?

.... [1]

b What characteristic is most important for everyone at the school?

.... [1]

2 **a** What did the girl find difficult about baking a cake?

.... [1]

b How does the girl describe the cake she made?

.... [1]

3 **a** Which part of the new bike did the boy have a big problem with?

.... [1]

b Where does the boy regularly cycle to?

.... [1]

4 **a** What does the woman think is the most impressive thing about a golden eagle?

.... [1]

b What is the main food eaten by golden eagles?

.... [1]

[Total: 8]

Audio for the listening exercises is on the CDs and online at cambridge.org/education/igcse-esl-tests.

Exercise 2

🔊 **CD2 audio track 15**

5   You will hear a talk given by a young woman called Christina Lawson, who's taken up gardening as a new hobby. Listen to the talk and complete the sentences below. Write **one** or **two** words only in each gap.

You will hear the talk twice.

Gardening

.... were the first things that Christina successfully grew in her garden.

Christina admits that .... is a job she doesn't enjoy.

Christina was sad that .... ruined some plants she particularly loved.

She has found out that .... can be good for plants.

Christina wanted a .... in the garden, though her family weren't keen.

Christina's family also built a .... to replace something else in the garden.

In the future, Christina hopes to have a .... garden.

Christina is considering a career as a ....

[Total: 8]

Audio for the listening exercises is on the CDs and online at cambridge.org/education/igcse-esl-tests.

Exercise 3

🔊 **CD2 audio track 16**

6 You will hear six people talking about their experiences of visiting famous tourist attractions. For each of Speakers 1 to 6, choose from the list, **A** to **G**, which opinion each speaker expresses. Write the letter in the appropriate box. Use each letter only once. There is one extra letter which you do not need to use.

You will hear the recordings twice.

Speaker 1 ☐   **A**   It took too long for me to see everything.

Speaker 2 ☐   **B**   It made me feel some strong emotions.

Speaker 3 ☐   **C**   It was difficult to get there.

Speaker 4 ☐   **D**   It was very different from what I'd expected.

Speaker 5 ☐   **E**   It was so crowded that I couldn't enjoy being there.

Speaker 6 ☐   **F**   It was very good value for money.

　　　　　　　　　 G   It had excellent facilities for visitors.

[Total: 6]

Audio for the listening exercises is on the CDs and online at cambridge.org/education/igcse-esl-tests.

Please turn over for Question 7.

Exercise 4

CD2 audio track 17

7   You will hear an interview with a man called Alex Murray, an actor who works in the theatre. Listen to the interview and look at the questions.

For each question, choose the correct answer, **A, B** or **C**, and put a tick (✓) in the appropriate box.

You will hear the interview twice.

a   Alex says that being on stage is more enjoyable for him because

    A   it gives him a greater sense of achievement. ☐

    B   the pressure he feels makes him perform better. ☐

    C   he gets immediate feedback on how he is doing. ☐ [1]

b   When Alex was given his first acting part in a school play

    A   he was excited to be given such an opportunity. ☐

    B   nobody seemed to mind that he didn't perform well. ☐

    C   it was because his friend had recommended him. ☐ [1]

c   What is Alex's attitude to the auditions he attends?

    A   He gets annoyed by the way they are organised. ☐

    B   He accepts them as something he cannot avoid. ☐

    C   He is confident he can predict whether he will be successful. ☐ [1]

d   How does Alex prepare when he gets a new part?

    A He depends on his imagination to create the character.   ☐

    B He studies other actors who have had the same role.   ☐

    C He talks to other actors in the play about their roles.   ☐   [1]

e   What does Alex say about learning his lines?

    A It is only possible if he works closely with others.   ☐

    B It is not something that causes many difficulties.   ☐

    C It is easier for him to do it at a particular time.   ☐   [1]

f   What does he say about working with directors?

    A He is willing to accept most of their ideas.   ☐

    B He believes some can waste time discussing details.   ☐

    C He can find their different approaches confusing.   ☐   [1]

g   When Alex wears his costume for the first time,

    A he often thinks again about the character he's going to play.   ☐

    B he tends to ask for changes to be made immediately.   ☐

    C he begins to feel nervous about the play for the first time.   ☐   [1]

h   How does Alex feel about the reviews of the plays he is in?

    A He is aware that he can learn something from them.   ☐

    B He doubts that the journalists understand the theatre.   ☐

    C He is annoyed that they focus on the negative points.   ☐   [1]

[Total: 8]

Audio for the listening exercises is on the CDs and online at cambridge.org/education/igcse-esl-tests.

Exercise 5

🔊 **CD2 audio track 18**

8 a You will hear a teacher giving a talk about the history of toys. Listen to the talk and complete the notes in part **(a)**. Write **one** or **two** words only. You will hear the talk twice.

The history of toys

It's remarkable that .... were created thousands of years ago, and were quite technically advanced.

In the 1700s toys such as .... were given to children to improve their knowledge of the world.

The teacher thinks it's great that children could even use toy .... when playing with their dolls houses.

At the beginning of the 1900s toys known as .... appealed to many children.

Currently, more and more .... are sold as toys in order to give publicity to television series or films.

[5]

Audio for the listening exercises is on the CDs and online at cambridge.org/education/igcse-esl-tests.

CD2 audio track 19

8 b Now listen to a conversation between two students about their visit to the toy museum and complete the sentences in part **(b)**. Write **one** or **two** words only in each gap. You will hear the conversation twice.

Visiting the toy museum

The students didn't realise how old .... was.

The girl says she studied the exhibit made from .... in great detail.

The boy appreciated the .... – one of the many toys that was produced after the first Moon landing.

One of the earliest electronic games, known as the .... , had an educational purpose.

Both students didn't enjoy listening to the museum guide talking about ....

[5]

[Total: 10]

Speaking – topic cards

A	Healthy lifestyle
B	Football
C	People around us
D	The right time and the wrong time
E	Comparing
F	24 hours a day
G	Dreaming
H	Nurses and doctors
I	Being thoughtful
J	Inspiration

© Cambridge University Press 2018

A   Healthy lifestyle

More and more people nowadays want to lead a healthy life by eating healthily and staying active.

Discuss this topic with the examiner.

Use the following prompts, in the order given below, to develop the conversation:

- how you, or people you know, keep fit[1]
- whether it is easy to get healthy food nowadays[2]
- the challenges of leading a healthy lifestyle[3]
- the suggestion that happiness in life is more important than a healthy lifestyle[4]
- the view that people who don't lead a healthy lifestyle cause problems in society.[5]

You may introduce **related** ideas of your own to expand on these prompts.

Remember, you are not allowed to make any written notes.

1 **Think about the following:**
- what you do / how often / when you started and why
- whether you, and your friends keep fit enough

2 **Think about the following:**
- the cost / the availability / the range
- what the situation was for your parents' generation / will be in the future

3 **Think about the following:**
- the cost / the time needed to do this
- how people's jobs affect their health

4 **Think about the following:**
- whether people who don't keep fit are happier because they have more free time
- whether people are too obsessed with healthy lifestyles nowadays

5 **Think about the following:**
- examples of poor lifestyles and the consequences of this (e.g. busy hospitals)

B   Football

Football is a popular sport all over the world because anyone can play it.

Discuss this topic with the examiner.

Use the following prompts, in the order given below, to develop the conversation:

- whether you like football, and why
- reasons why more boys play football than girls[2]
- the pros and cons of watching football live at a stadium[3]
- the view that footballers make good role models for young people[4]
- the suggestion that the top football clubs are more interested in money than the sport itself.[5]

You may introduce **related** ideas of your own to expand on these prompts.

Remember, you are not allowed to make any written notes.

2   Think about the following:

- agree – give reasons why more boys prefer this game and whether this will change in the future
- disagree – give examples of girls' teams (e.g. at your school, national teams)

3   Think about the following:

- the atmosphere / the cost / how busy the stadium gets / how much people can see
- compare with watching matches on TV

4   Think about the following:

- whether you agree/disagree, and why
- footballers' behaviour / charity work
- what positive characteristics young people learn from footballers

5   Think about the following:

- whether football has become a business rather than a sport (agree/disagree)
- whether it is right for football clubs to pay a lot of money for foreign players

C   People around us

In our lives we are surrounded by a range of people from family and friends to complete strangers.

Discuss this topic with the examiner.

Use the following prompts, in the order given below, to develop the conversation:

- people you meet every day and what you talk about
- whether you find it difficult to meet new people, and why
- the pros and cons of being surrounded by a lot of different people[3]
- the view that younger people don't spend enough time with older people[4]
- the suggestion that in the future we will be surrounded mainly by robots, but not human beings.[5]

You may introduce **related** ideas of your own to expand on these prompts.

Remember, you are not allowed to make any written notes.

3   Think about the following:

- what you prefer personally, and why
- how people feel being surrounded by others / being alone
- what things are better done with other people / on your own, and why

4   Think about the following:

- how much time you spend with older generations yourself and whether it's enough
- whether young people spend more/less time with older people than in the past, and why
- what you can learn from older people and how important this is

5   Think about the following:

- whether we'll still live with / meet face to face with other people
- whether robots can replace human beings in everyday life situations (e.g. cleaning jobs, teaching, office jobs, caring for others, as companions)
- what life will be like / how people will feel if we are surrounded by robots only

D   The right time and the wrong time

Some things in life, for example, getting a job offer, happen at the right time, some don't.

Discuss this topic with the examiner.

Use the following prompts, in the order given below, to develop the conversation:

- a time when something happened at the wrong time for you
- whether there is a right time for young people to move out of their parents' house
- the pros and cons of waiting for the right time to do something important
- the importance of saying the right thing at the right time[4]
- the view that people can't control the time when certain things happen in life.[5]

You may introduce **related** ideas of your own to expand on these prompts.

Remember, you are not allowed to make any written notes.

4 **Think about the following:**
- general examples of situations when people need to be careful about what they say and how they say it (e.g. the way somebody looks, answers at job interviews, when somebody is feeling sad about something)
- times when it was difficult for you, or your friends, to say the right thing and why
- whether advice is always accepted well by other people, and why

5 **Think about the following:**
- examples of things people hope to achieve in life (e.g. get rich very young, pass exams, go travelling, buy something special) and whether these things always happen the way/when people want them to happen

E   Comparing

People often compare how similar or different their lives are with other people's lives.

Discuss this topic with the examiner.

Use the following prompts, in the order given below, to develop the conversation:

- how similar or different you are to your friends
- reasons why young people compare themselves to others
- the opinion that parents shouldn't compare their children to each other
- the view that people will always compare their lives with somebody who is rich and famous
- the suggestion that people would be much happier if they stopped comparing themselves to other people.[5]

You may introduce **related** ideas of your own to expand on these prompts.

Remember, you are not allowed to make any written notes.

F   24 hours a day

People in our modern society spend most of the day working and have less and less time to do the things they enjoy.

Discuss this topic with the examiner.

Use the following prompts, in the order given below, to develop the conversation:

- a time when you had a really busy day, and what happened
- whether young people have enough free time nowadays, and why
- the reasons why our modern society is getting busier
- the suggestion that shops and restaurants should be open 24 hours a day
- the view that our busy lifestyles have a negative impact on families and the whole society.

You may introduce **related** ideas of your own to expand on these prompts.

Remember, you are not allowed to make any written notes.

5 Think about the following:

- how people feel when they compare themselves to others, and why
- reasons why people compare themselves with others
- the pressure of advertising to have certain things / to look a certain way
- whether nobody is ever happy with the things they have / the way they look

---

G   Dreaming

We often dream when we're sleeping at night, but we can also dream during the day about our future plans.

Discuss this topic with the examiner.

Use the following prompts, in the order given below, to develop the conversation:

- a time you had a dream while you were sleeping, and what it was about
- what kind of dreams about the future young people have these days
- the opinion that people have to work very hard to make their dreams come true
- the view that people nowadays often have unrealistic dreams about their future
- the suggestion that a life without dreams would be very empty.

You may introduce **related** ideas of your own to expand on these prompts.

Remember, you are not allowed to make any written notes.

H   Doctors and nurses

Doctors and nurses have a very important job to save lives and to look after sick people in hospitals.

Discuss this topic with the examiner.

Use the following prompts, in the order given below, to develop the conversation:

- whether you would like to be a doctor or a nurse, and why
- the pros and cons of working as a doctor or a nurse
- the opinion that the work of doctors and nurses is not valued enough
- the view that nurses work much harder than doctors do
- the view that governments should never cut money spent on hospitals.

You may introduce **related** ideas of your own to expand on these prompts.

Remember, you are not allowed to make any written notes.

I   Being thoughtful

Thoughtful people are kind and always try to help others.

Discuss this topic with the examiner.

Use the following prompts, in the order given below, to develop the conversation:

- a time you did something thoughtful for other people
- how often other people are thoughtful to you, and what they do
- times when it is difficult to be thoughtful, and why
- the opinion that our modern society is making people less and less thoughtful
- the view that thoughtful people make bad leaders.

You may introduce **related** ideas of your own to expand on these prompts.

Remember, you are not allowed to make any written notes.

J   Inspiration

We can be inspired by things we see, hear or read. We can also be inspired by other people and their actions.

Discuss this topic with the examiner.

Use the following prompts, in the order given below, to develop the conversation:

- a person that has inspired you, and why
- whether things like music or books can inspire people, and how
- ways parents and schools can inspire young children
- the opinion that young people are only inspired by contemporary artists, not by people from the past
- the view that politicians should try to inspire more young people to go into politics.

You may introduce **related** ideas of your own to expand on these prompts.

Remember, you are not allowed to make any written notes.

© Cambridge University Press 2018

Audioscripts

Practice Test 1

CD1 Track 02

Exercise 1

You will hear four short recordings. Answer **each** question on the line provided. Write no more than three words for each answer.

You will hear each recording twice.

Question 1

(a) **What new thing does the girl have in her room?**

(b) **What is the girl going to do next to improve her room?**

V1 Your room looks a bit different from last time. Have you done anything to it?

V2 Well, I was fed up with how it looked. To be honest, I want to change everything if I can, even the carpet! My parents suggested replacing my desk. I said I was more interested in getting a better cupboard. What I had before was too small. The new one is more suitable for all my files.

V1 Are you going to do anything else?

V2 I was thinking of moving my bed nearer to the window, but I changed my mind. Dad offered to paint my walls because they really need doing. I asked if I could do it. I start next weekend! I might change the curtains … if I can persuade my mum.

{ ping }

Now listen to the recording again.

CD1 Track 03

Question 2

(a) **What was the man most worried about before the race?**

(b) **What does the man think is the reason for his good result?**

V1 How did the race go?

V2 I wasn't very confident before the race, but then again, I never am! Most runners worry about starting well, but that's one of my strengths. I was more concerned about the weather – it really wasn't ideal for running. The crowd were noisy which can be distracting, but it didn't bother me.

V1 And did you win?

V2 No, I only came third, but my time was the best I've ever managed. I'd done plenty of extra training, but I don't think it made much difference actually. I reckon eating more pasta was the key thing. In the past I'd eaten other things before races.

{ ping }

Now listen to the recording again.

CD1 Track 04

Question 3

(a) **What does the boy think is special about the songs by his favourite singer?**

(b) **Why was the boy disappointed by the concert given by his favourite singer?**

V1 I've been listening to some new songs by my favourite singer – she's called Elena. Do you know her?

V2 I think so, isn't she the one who writes those unusual lyrics?

V1 Actually, they aren't what appeals to me most; it's the different styles she can do that make her stand out. I enjoy everything she does.

V2 Did you see her concert on TV?

V1 Yes. She had an orchestra, which was not what I expected but it was cool. The trouble was the sound quality. It wasn't quite right. I don't know if it was the venue or my TV. The backing singers were OK, and I disagree with the online criticism of them.

{ ping }

Now listen to the recording again.

CD1 Track 05

Question 4

(a) **What does the woman say was difficult about organising the birthday party?**

(b) **What pleased her grandad most about the party?**

V1 Did your grandfather's party go well?

V2 Great, thanks. I was in charge of organising everything. I thought choosing a date might be tricky, but in the end most people were free on grandad's birthday. And of course buying food was a real challenge! There was so much to think about.

V1 Did your grandad enjoy the party?

V2 Yes, he got a lot of presents. I don't know if he was expecting that because he didn't say. Seeing old friends really put a smile on his face. The party was over too soon really, but at least grandad had a chance to do some dancing!

{ ping }

Now listen to the recording again.

CD1 Track 06

Exercise 2

You will hear a talk given by a man who visited the Baja Desert in Mexico. Listen to the talk and complete the sentences below. Write one or two words only in each gap.

You will hear the talk twice.

V1 My name's Tom Duncan and I'm going to tell you about my trip to the Baja Desert in Mexico. It's surrounded by the Sea of Cortez on the one side and the Pacific Ocean on the other. The popular holiday resorts in the south of the desert are full of tourists. Playing golf is what attracts many of them while others come to do deep-sea fishing. The Pacific coast is one of the best places in the world for watching whales, which was what I did before anything else.

The coast is absolutely stunning. On the following day I thought about sunbathing or having picnics on a wonderful beach with white sand. Sea kayaking was possible, something I was sure would be fun because I'd done it before. In the end I opted to go diving. After all, the Sea of Cortez is known as the aquarium of the world!

It was now time to explore the desert. I wanted to take no risks so I hired a guide. I already had a good sun hat which I'd worn on previous trips to hot places. But at the last moment I had to invest in some walking shoes. Maps and guide books may be helpful for some people out in the desert, but with my highly experienced guide I didn't have to worry about anything.

The desert is an astonishing but strange place. People have said that it's like being on the surface of an alien planet. I've also read descriptions of the Baja in which people compared their first view of it to a prehistoric scene – something from millions of years ago. Actually, the place made me think of a cowboy film; it had that sort of atmosphere.

Everywhere you can see cacti – the typical desert plant. I couldn't believe the age of several cacti we came across. I was told they were five hundred years old. The size of the cacti is worth mentioning too as they can reach 25 metres in height.

There are many other interesting plants there. I knew that some desert plants are edible and can be used as food. I'd also read that other plants were a source of medicine for the people living in the Baja centuries ago. My guide even told me in particular about one common bush that provided a natural sunblock. It was probably just as effective as the chemical products used today!

The desert is famous for its rare wildlife. I glimpsed a golden eagle several times, but catching sight of something like a kangaroo rat, which I really wanted to see, didn't happen, unfortunately. I was told seeing a rock squirrel would be a challenge, but my guide pointed out several during our trip.

Just a day before the end of the holiday, I visited the El Vizcaion reserve where there are some rock paintings. These were done by people who lived in the Baja thousands of years ago and are some of the best preserved examples in the whole world. In the coastal towns there is some interesting architecture, but it didn't appeal to me much because it was similar to what I'd seen in other places.

I had a great time and I'd love to return there one day.

{ ping }

Now listen to the talk again.

CD1 Track 07

Exercise 3

You will hear six students talking about experiments they did in science lessons. For each of Speakers 1 to 6, choose from the list, A to G, which opinion each speaker expresses. Write the letter in the appropriate box. Use each letter only once. There is one extra letter which you do not need to use.

You will hear the recordings twice.

Speaker 1

V1 I've never been that keen on chemistry or physics and doing experiments in the laboratory. I'm always nervous about messing everything up. However, on this particular day we'd come up with some really accurate data which the teacher said was impressive. It was way beyond what I'd expected at the start, so that was a real bonus. I think we were successful because everyone in my group really knew what they were doing, which was great. We weren't close friends but we got on together well enough.

Speaker 2

V2 I'm much more into chemistry than I used to be and am pretty confident about doing experiments. A couple of my mates had done a similar experiment last year and gave me some useful tips. It was a tough exercise for some in the class, but I thought the subject matter was easy to grasp. The problem was getting the equipment ready; we wasted some time checking that things were working. This meant we did the experiment in a rush and we were disappointed at the poor results.

Speaker 3

V3   I was working with a group of people I didn't know very well but that didn't matter because I was just concentrating on the work we had to do. Although we got things set up efficiently without taking up too much time, I managed to break a glass test tube, which wasn't the best of starts. Then I realised I'd misunderstood the instructions. The funny thing was that all this didn't hold us back much and the results were OK and in line with what we expected.

Speaker 4

V4   I wasn't sure I fully understood what we were doing because I've always struggled with physics. There's no doubt that it was complicated – even my classmates who are brilliant at the subject said so. Fortunately I was working with my friends which made the whole experience more enjoyable. Things didn't quite go according to plan and so our results were inaccurate. Actually, I understand the theory behind this experiment more clearly now, though that doesn't mean I've suddenly decided I love physics!

Speaker 5

V5   My friends and I all prefer things like history and literature, so science lessons aren't something we normally look forward to. But last week we did a chemistry experiment which was fairly straightforward. I could understand what we were doing and why. I managed to avoid making the sort of mistakes that usually let me down, and at the end of the lesson I felt a sense of achievement. For once I could see the point of what we are doing and how science can help you test a theory.

Speaker 6

V6   I usually enjoy science lessons because I get to work with my friends and have a laugh – though we always get the work done. We're good at preparing carefully, even if it takes us a while. I'm usually in charge when we're doing experiments because I'm slightly better at science and maths than them. This time they kept telling me that I was heating the chemicals up too strongly, but I was convinced I was right. In fact, the results turned out all wrong. I think I learnt a lesson there!

{ ping }

Now listen to the six speakers again.

CD1 Track 08

Exercise 4

You will hear an interview with a woman called Jo Baylis, who is a radio presenter. Listen to the interview and look at the questions. For each question, choose the correct answer, A, B or C, and put a tick in the appropriate box.

You will hear the interview twice.

V1   Today we're talking to Jo Baylis, who presents a programme on City Radio. Jo, have you always wanted to be a radio presenter?

V2   Not really. When I was young I was a fan of what was at the time a very popular radio programme, though it didn't inspire me to become a presenter myself. I'd heard that to work on the radio you have to be extrovert and funny, which wasn't really me. But I remember that one day my father was interviewed on the radio and I found that thrilling. It sparked an interest in becoming a presenter.

V1   So how did your first ever radio show go?

V2   Not too well, to be honest! I was working at a local radio station, and I had to tell the listeners about a festival. I planned for ages but only had a few minutes to get across a lot of information and I made plenty of mistakes – like talking too fast - and that was down to getting little instruction or coaching from anyone, which was a shame. Nerves are often a big issue for beginners but I felt relaxed.

V1   So what sort of programmes do you like to do?

V2   Well, I'm passionate about music, and it would be fun to play songs by famous bands and talk about them. But actually I prefer to do something more interactive like having debates on all sorts of subjects with my listeners. I host a programme where I do exactly that. I was recently offered a programme chatting about cinema and soap operas, but I turned it down!

V1   Your programme is on quite early in the morning. Is that a problem?

V2   It was a struggle at first, though I've learnt to adapt. Now it feels normal to be up at five o'clock and even before a strong coffee I'm pretty cheerful. Doing this job means going to bed really early too, and that can very occasionally stop me going out with friends. But since I've always had a quiet life, this job hasn't made much of a difference overall.

V1   How important is it that you get a positive response from your listeners?

V2 It's essential they appreciate what I'm doing. I get lots of feedback every day, but I can't please everyone all the time, or take into account everything people say. It's amazing how listeners see things in so many different ways. I get comments and reactions that I don't expect. People are usually very nice, even if they are being critical of the content of the programme, which by the way I don't mind. People have the right to complain.

V1 Would you say you've got a difficult job?

V2 It's hard to produce the show, do all the research *and* present it. On the other hand, I quite like having so much responsibility. The real challenge is being original. Every week I need a new topic and that's tough sometimes. As for the pressure of staying alert and focused every time I'm on air, that's less of an issue.

V1 How do you feel when you sit there talking to an audience you can't see?

V2 Actually, I feel like I'm in conversation with my mates in a coffee bar or something. People say it must feel strange talking even though you don't have anyone there in front of you, but that's not a feeling that lasted long in my case. How I am when I'm on the radio is exactly how I am at home; I'm natural and I don't put on an act or anything.

V1 Do you hope to become a TV presenter one day?

V2 Well, if you know where to look, there are opportunities to make a move into TV. But it's probably a mistake to think a radio presenter can just walk into a TV studio and be fine. I've seen talented radio presenters who've struggled. It's been embarrassing to watch. Although I reckon I'd be OK, I'm perfectly suited to what I'm doing right now, and the way forward is to get better at it rather than try something new.

{ ping }

Now listen to the interview again.

CD1 Track 09

Exercise 5 part (a)

You will hear a science teacher called Mr Hamilton giving a talk about asteroids which are rocky worlds revolving around the Sun. Listen to the talk and complete the notes in part (a). Write one or two words only.

You will hear the talk twice.

V1 I'm very interested in astronomy which, as you probably know, is the science concerned with the universe – space and all the different objects out there. The solar system, which the Earth is part of,

is very complex, and there are many different types of object contained within it. In my opinion, the most interesting are the asteroids, which are rocky worlds orbiting the Sun, mostly between Mars and Jupiter. They're all much smaller than the Earth, and usually lack the characteristics of comets which are mostly ice and dust. They are classified as minor planets, which is the most frequent term applied, though you do occasionally hear others such as 'planetoid'.

Asteroids vary in size, with the largest approximately 1000 kilometres across. They are thought to be pieces of rock left over from the formation of the solar system 4.6 billion years ago. Now when it comes to the form they take, most of them are irregular and so rather different from the spherical nature of planets like the Earth. Asteroids are often heavily cratered – craters are holes on the surface of an asteroid or planet where it's collided with other pieces of rock.

The more I read about asteroids, the more I appreciated just how different they can be. Some have tails composed of gas which makes them look like comets, and there is even one with its own set of rings around it. It's astonishing that about 150 actually have moons, just like many of the planets do. There are also double asteroids which travel through space as a pair!

Asteroids are all made of rock but the precise type varies considerably. The classification is complex so I won't give you all the details here, but some are strange colours like green. The largest group of asteroids are known as 'C-type' and are grey. Most of these are in the outer regions of the asteroid belt and so are the most distant from the Earth. Then there are the 'M-type' asteroids which are mainly red.

There are thousands of asteroids out there and all are given an official number, but many have names too. Originally the asteroids were named after mythological figures such as gods and goddesses, but now it seems they can get the names of celebrities which I don't think is right. Some are named after places on the Earth and that seems a bit more reasonable to me!

{ ping }

Now listen to the talk again.

CD1 Track 10

Exercise 5 part (b)

Now listen to a conversation between two students about asteroids and complete the sentences in part (b). Write one or two words, or a number, in each gap.

You will hear the conversation twice.

V1   That talk on asteroids was quite interesting, wasn't it? There were a few things the teacher wanted us to do some research on, so what did you find out?

V2   Well, fragments of an asteroid can hit the Earth. I've read that many measuring between one and ten metres enter the atmosphere every day, but they all burn up at an altitude of about 50 kilometres, and don't do any harm. It's the ones bigger than about 30 metres that can cause serious damage.

V1   And imagine the problems that might be caused by an asteroid nearer to 5 kilometres in diameter!

V2   So it's quite important to know exactly where all the asteroids are.

V1   Yes. I read that the first ones were discovered as early as the 19th century with telescopes. Ceres, the very first asteroid, was initially mistaken for a star. But the scientist realised that its position was slightly different each night and so couldn't be a star.

V2   Right. And in the 1890s cameras were used for the first time. Pictures of a large area of space could now be taken and new asteroids discovered. After 1998, special computers were used.

V1   Have we sent spacecraft to any asteroids yet? I didn't find anything about that.

V2   Yes, in 1991 we got the first images of an asteroid from an American spacecraft called Galileo. Then in 2006 a similar Japanese craft – or probe as they are usually called – landed on another asteroid and brought back rock samples for scientists to study. That was a major development.

V1   I've read that asteroids could be important in the future.

V2   It's unlikely we'll ever set up colonies and live on asteroids, though.

V1   But mining the asteroids could be important because we're running out of raw materials such as metals and minerals on Earth. I expected there to be metal on the asteroids because I've read that they're often composed of iron. There's almost certainly zinc and tin on some of them too, but I couldn't believe it when I read that rare metals are likely to be found under the surface too.

V2   Yeah, that's amazing.

V1   Asteroids might provide rocket fuel, which is the most important consideration for space exploration. That's because some asteroids contain hydrogen and oxygen in the form of ice, and other things like

ammonia, which could be used to power spacecraft, as well as making other chemicals like fertilisers to help plants grow on other planets. This is probably less important in the short term, however.

V2   This all sounds like science fiction but one day it could be science fact!

{ ping }

Now listen to the conversation again.

Practice Test 2
CD1 Track 11
Exercise 1

You will hear four short recordings. Answer each question on the line provided. Write no more than three words for each answer.

You will hear each recording twice.

Question 1

(a)   What subject is the girl's online blog about?

(b)   What does the girl find most difficult about blogging?

V1   So you've started a blog, haven't you?

V2   Yes, it's a web page where I express my opinions and people comment on what I say. My original idea was to write about sport.

V1   That sounds like a great idea.

V2   Well, I know several friends who are doing that so I changed my mind. I considered a blog about films, but in the end I opted for fashion, even though there are lots of similar blogs.

V1   Is it hard?

V2   Well, the technical side is fine once you get started. Finding new ideas is a real challenge, though. Some bloggers dislike dealing with comments left by people who read their blog. For me it's usually a pleasure.

{ ping }

Now listen to the recording again.

CD1 Track 12
Question 2

(a)   What did the boy paint for the art competition he entered?

(b)   How did the judges describe the painting the boy did?

V1: Recently I won first prize in an art competition. I did the painting quite quickly. Initially I thought of doing a landscape. It was a view from my grandparents' house. I gave that idea up and then I didn't know what to do. Painting a person – like my dad, for example – was something above my level really. Painting a cat though wasn't challenging at all. I was quite pleased with it. People said the other competition entries were more imaginative and a few were described as really unusual. But maybe that wasn't quite what the judges wanted. They said mine was very professional, which made me so proud!

{ ping }

Now listen to the recording again.

CD1 Track 13

Question 3

(a) **What did the boy learn about chocolate when he was at the factory?**

(b) **What type of flavour did the boy have in his chocolate bar?**

V1 I visited a chocolate factory the other day. It was a lot of fun!

V2 Did you learn anything new?

V1 Well, I already knew about the production of chocolate because we'd studied it at school once, but I wasn't at all familiar with the history involved. I'd like to find out more about how they made and ate chocolate hundreds of years ago in other cultures.

V2 Did you get to taste any chocolate?

V1 Yes! I actually had a go at choosing a filling for a chocolate bar. In the end I went for honey. My friend had suggested peanut butter at first, though orange and ginger appealed to me too.

V2 They all sound great!

{ ping }

Now listen to the recording again.

CD1 Track 14

Question 4

(a) **What new clothes did the girl buy for herself?**

(b) **What did the girl dislike about the shop?**

V1 So did you go to that new clothes shop?

V2 Yes. I had to help my cousin choose a couple of new dresses. There was so much choice! I was hoping to find some new trousers and tried on several pairs. I'd nearly decided what to buy when I got distracted by some T-shirts. I couldn't resist buying two!

V1 Is it a good shop?

V2 Yes. In most shops the sales assistants are annoying. At least in this new shop they just let you browse. The music was loud though. It was hard to hear myself think. I can't say the prices were a problem. They were quite reasonable compared to other places in town.

{ ping }

Now listen to the recording again.

CD1 Track 15

Exercise 2

You will hear a talk given by a man called Josh Collins, who helped organise a carnival in his town. Listen to the talk and complete the sentences below. Write one or two words only in each gap.

You will hear the talk twice.

V1 My name's Josh Collins and I'm going to tell you about a carnival that I helped to organise in my town. It's usually held in August because this is the month when the weather is generally best. However, this year we had to move the date to June. Some colleagues had suggested May and we did consider it for a while before going for the later date.

Carnivals are famous for their music and so that was the first thing that we focused on when we were planning. A year ago we had a big jazz concert in the park, but this year we decided to move it to a different location and organise a rock concert there instead. The town hall hosted a smaller classical concert for those who appreciate a very different style of music!

There was a parade in the afternoon: hundreds of musicians and performers walked through the streets in amazing costumes, dancing and playing their instruments. This year we had bigger crowds than ever. The parade set off from the city gate and moved slowly down to the south beach. The route passed through the market, which has been a starting point in the past.

There were so many amazing performers this year that it's hard to say which one was most popular. The children loved the acrobats and there was a good response to the jugglers too. I wasn't surprised to hear the huge cheers for the samba dancers, though probably the drummers were the biggest success. They should appear again next year.

Everyone is encouraged to wear costumes for the carnival. Basically, people can wear what they like, but we do have a different theme each year. This time people were asked to dress as film characters which gave people quite a lot of freedom to express themselves. As usual, lots of people came to the carnival dressed up as animals. There were also some monsters, and for some reason this year we had quite a few pirates!

There were a number of stalls selling food and our aim was to have a really wide range of international cuisines represented, including of course Chinese, which is always in demand, and Indian. This year for the very first time we were able to offer Mexican food because so many people were disappointed last year that it wasn't one of the options. As usual, Italian food was also available, all prepared by some excellent chefs!

There was so much going on at the carnival it was difficult to know what to do on the big day. My wife was involved in the face-painting, so I made a brief visit there. However, from mid-morning I was in charge of the mini-golf, which was fun. I had time to check out other activities such as the bowling, and of course the football match, which was played to raise money for charity.

The carnival has to end in a spectacular way if at all possible. In the past we've had a funfair for the children. We rejected that idea this time around and decided on some fireworks as we thought this would appeal to the majority of people, whatever their age.

Overall, it went very well and I'm looking forward to continuing my involvement next year too!

{ ping }

Now listen to the talk again.

CD1 Track 16

Exercise 3

You will hear six people talking about their experiences of learning about history. For each of Speakers 1 to 6, choose from the list, A to G, which opinion each speaker expresses. Write the letter in the appropriate box. Use each letter only once. There is one extra letter which you do not need to use.

You will hear the recordings twice.

Speaker 1

V1   I went on a guided tour of a museum with my class. The guide was knowledgeable and a really positive and cheerful guy. He went into lots of detail on dates, something some students don't like, but I thought was helpful. Yet he also seemed to think that we knew a lot already, and when he gave the reasons why particular historical events had happened it was quite hard to follow. To be honest, at the end of the tour I didn't feel I particularly wanted to explore the subject in more depth!

Speaker 2

V2   We had a lesson on social history the other day – you know, studying how ordinary people lived in the past. The teacher also talked briefly about quite scientific aspects – things like health and diet for example. I got more of a sense of how when you study history you're studying everything. Some of my classmates said it was complicated and that you had to try very hard to follow everything, but I didn't agree. Our teacher was really dynamic and inspiring, though I think I was already excited about what we were doing. It was fascinating!

Speaker 3

V3   I went round a castle with a guide book. I had to walk quite a lot to find all the most interesting features. The guide book was probably too detailed but reading it carefully paid off because it meant I got so much more out of the visit. Some guide books are full of boring dates or are too technical, and so you don't fully understand what it's on about. Overall, the visit to the castle gave me a good impression of what it must have been like living in such a place.

Speaker 4

V4   At school I had to read some letters written in the 15th century. The language was different then so that was a challenge, but fortunately I had a teacher to help explain when necessary. And my friend was *really* into it, which was nice but didn't help me much. Reading these documents was supposed to show us how life in 1450 was completely different. With no illustrations in the book, it was a struggle to picture everything in my mind. I'm relieved that we won't be going any deeper into this subject next term.

Speaker 5

V5   I watched a documentary about the history of China which included loads of dates. Luckily, I'm good at remembering them! For the first time, I managed to make sense of how the world today is influenced by events that happened hundreds of years ago. Documentaries can give detailed explanations which leave you clueless, but the presenter was very clear. TV programmes are much better than books because you don't have to try and visualise everything – it's all there on the screen.

Speaker 6

V6   Yesterday I talked to my great-grandfather about his childhood. He's always keen to talk about the past. Of course, he's not an expert on the period he was growing up in so there are still plenty of gaps I'll have to fill by doing extra background research. His stories really brought the past to life so that I could imagine everything. The way he explains things can be difficult to follow sometimes but not this time. Many things were so different when he was young! And fortunately he didn't go on about dates very much.

{ ping }

Now listen to the six speakers again.

CD1 Track 17

Exercise 4

You will hear an interview with a woman called Rachel Smith, who is a sailor. Listen to the interview and look at the questions. For each question, choose the correct answer, A, B or C, and put a tick in the appropriate box.

You will hear the interview twice.

V1   Today we're talking to the successful young sailor Rachel Smith. What was your first experience of sailing like?

V2   A friend took me along to our local sailing club, and I wasn't very enthusiastic. I just attended to keep my best friend happy! But as I listened to the introductory talk, I thought sailing sounded more interesting than I'd expected. When we finally went out on a boat, I was full of nerves and was sure I'd get something wrong or fall in the water. It was OK though and my interest in sailing gradually grew from there.

V1   What was your first experience of being at sea and sailing for a longer period of time?

V2   When I was 16 I had a chance to be a crew member on a boat that was at sea for a week. I had a go at everything, including difficult technical things such as helping to put the sails up and even steering the boat for a short time. The more experienced crew members were very welcoming and also so patient when I needed help and support. They occasionally expected the less experienced crew members to do less exciting things like the washing up, but I didn't mind.

V1   Tell us about your very first boat. I heard it wasn't very big!

V2   Yes, it was very small actually. I was aware that other people certainly had boats with more facilities and better technology. However, I soon realised that I didn't need lots of space and a luxury cabin. In fact, it felt quite cosy in my boat. Small boats can be tricky to handle though, especially when you're sailing close to a rocky coast and so there is some risk, but mastering those techniques helped me when I got a much bigger boat.

V1   What are you looking for when you choose crew members?

V2   Well, it goes without saying that they should have the necessary skills, or else I wouldn't even bother interviewing them! If they're nice and have a good sense of humour that's a bonus, but I'm really hoping to find someone who's tough. Having a crew member who isn't discouraged or stressed when things aren't going well is essential.

V1   Two years ago you and your crew entered your first race. How did that go?

V2   Well, we decided to enter the competition only a few weeks before the race so it was a rush to prepare everything, though we managed it. We were up against some seriously good boats and experienced crews and they tested us to the limit. But I learnt how to handle storms and high winds, and I found that quite exciting, actually.

V1   You were very young when you started to race. How did other competitors react to you?

V2   They had watched my progress and so my success at such a young age wasn't a total surprise to the majority of them, though perhaps they were surprised by my self-belief. On the whole they were kind, and occasionally they even gave me a bit of informal advice. I don't think they wanted to be too nice though, because we were rivals and everyone wanted to win! Basically, we were studying each other's weak points so we could gain an advantage.

V1   This year you've started sailing alone for long periods. How does that feel?

V2   People say to me 'you must be terribly lonely' but I'm not too bothered about having to spend time on my own. If everything's quiet and the sea isn't rough then I read or chat to relatives on my satellite link, though I prefer not to do that too often because it's a distraction, to be honest. Generally, I'm simply too busy with the boat to feel down or anxious.

V1 You recently won a race across the Atlantic to the United States. Tell me about that.

V2 It was a great achievement for me. I'd had problems with faulty equipment which were only resolved at the last minute, so I went into the race less relaxed than usual. I managed on only four hours sleep a night, with naps during the day. Somehow I found the strength to keep focused mentally throughout the race, especially at those points when making the right decision was vital!

{ ping }

Now listen to the interview again.

CD1 Track 18

Exercise 5 part (a)

You will hear a man called Eddie Granger giving a talk about his visit to a place called the Butterfly Centre. Listen to the talk and complete the notes in part (a). Write one or two words only.

You will hear the talk twice.

V1 The other day I visited a very interesting tourist attraction called the Butterfly Centre in the south west of England. Here you can see hundreds of butterflies from the tropical rainforests of places like Central America. Great efforts are made to create the right conditions for these delicate creatures, and protect them from the British climate outside. Ensuring the temperature is right is less of a challenge than maintaining the right humidity. The lighting is important, but isn't so much of a technical issue.

I had a conversation with a staff member there and she explained what a demanding job it was. There's so much to do, with watering flowers taking up a considerable amount of her time. Another important task is feeding the butterflies – this involves carefully preparing fruit and placing it on tables where the butterflies then gather. However, she said she was mainly in charge of examining these beautiful creatures. This is done for medical reasons. Treating the butterflies for any disease that is found was the job of another highly qualified colleague.

In every part of the centre there is lots of vegetation, including the lady palm, which creates the feeling of a tropical rain forest. There are mango trees and a few guava trees, and I was told there were some coffee plants too, though I didn't see any. In one section there was an enormous number of banana plants, which I didn't expect – apparently many butterfly species lay their eggs on these leaves and the caterpillars consume them. Other species of butterfly are much fussier about what they eat – for example, the Tiger Longwing will only lay their eggs on the vines of passion flowers.

When you walk around the centre you have to be careful not to step on any butterflies. This is because they spend time on the ground drinking the moisture. Visitors are surprised when they're reminded to walk slowly to minimise the problem of sound vibrations caused by walking around, which is something people aren't always aware of. It goes without saying that you shouldn't touch any of them as their wings are so fragile.

There's a range of facilities at the centre. It also runs guided tours, though these aren't essential because of the information boards everywhere. The staff also hand out educational leaflets on particular butterflies which are particularly informative and taught me a lot, and it's possible to attend a couple of lectures before going around the centre. But I realise something that formal might not suit everyone.

{ ping }

Now listen to the talk again.

CD1 Track 19

Exercise 5 part (b)

Now listen to a conversation between two students about attracting butterflies to gardens and complete the sentences in part (b). Write one or two words only in each gap.

You will hear the conversation twice.

V1 How did your research on butterflies go? I've read that many species are endangered. Some scientists have blamed pollution, though no definite link has been made. It doesn't seem to be the result of climate change because that's actually helped some species. It's mainly because of habitat loss. But even an urban garden can be set up to attract butterflies and so help them survive.

V2 Yes, and from what I've read the size of the garden is irrelevant. It seemed logical to me that a garden will be more attractive to butterflies if it offers warmth, though that's not something you can control unfortunately. What's less obvious to people is that butterflies require shelter, especially when the weather's not brilliant.

V1 And of course having a supply of nectar is essential, so you need a variety of flowers – biodiversity is the key.

V2 That's right. There's one interesting thing my grandmother does to encourage butterflies in her garden. After pears become ripe and fall from the trees in the late summer and autumn, she doesn't pick them up because butterflies can feed on the sugar inside them. She also says butterflies like to settle on flat stones so they can rest and sunbathe, though she hasn't put any out so far. She has a plan to make two small ponds as they could also attract butterflies.

V2   Yes, that's a good idea.

V1   And according to scientific research, pesticides harm butterflies, so scientists don't think they should be used in the garden. What I didn't know – and I guess this might be a problem for some gardeners – is that a slightly wild garden, especially at the edges, is great for butterflies. Cutting lawns is fine, though.

V2   I'm curious to know what sort of butterflies might turn up in my garden so I've checked in a reference book.

V1   Well, apparently there are 59 species in Britain with about 30 others that are migrants, so you can see them very occasionally.

V2   Well, I guess everyone has seen a Cabbage White. Unfortunately they tend to eat the vegetables you're growing! Another common but much more beautiful butterfly is the Red Admiral. I've been trying to get a close look at the Orange Tip with no success so far. They're much less likely to appear in a garden. The Small Copper is quite rare and I don't expect to ever spot one. It doesn't quite have the same appeal to me anyway.

{ ping }

Now listen to the conversation again.

Practice Test 3

CD2 Track 02

Exercise 1

You will hear four short recordings. Answer each question on the line provided. Write no more than three words for each answer.

You will hear each recording twice.

Question 1

(a)   Where was the fashion show held?

(b)   Why does the girl think the fashion show was successful?

V1   I hear the fashion show went well on Saturday.

V2   Yes, it was great. We'd been planning for it to take place at the college. We soon realised

there wasn't enough space. The town hall would've been perfect except for the cost, so we booked the sports centre and attracted a big crowd there.

V1   Why do you think the show was a success?

V2   To be honest, the cheap tickets were probably the reason things went so well. The advertising can make a difference too. This time we probably didn't do enough, but it didn't matter in the end. Most years we have unusual designs which appeal to everyone, though this year we had far fewer like that.

{ ping }

Now listen to the recording again.

CD2 Track 03

Question 2

(a)   Where does the cartoon film begin?

(b)   Why does the man think the cartoon will be popular?

V1   Here's Mike Peters with a review of the latest cartoon film, *Grandpa Superhero*.

V2   This animated film is aimed at the whole family. Unlike the previous highly successful film in the series that features an American city, it's mostly set in Australia, though there is a rather surprising opening scene at the North Pole. It's an imaginative plot though unnecessarily complicated perhaps. The amusing script makes up for any problems the film may have, and will guarantee the film's success at the box office. The characters are probably what audiences would expect from this type of movie.

{ ping }

Now listen to the recording again.

CD2 Track 04

Question 3

(a)   What impressed the girl most about the football match?

(b)   How does the boy describe the captain of the team?

V1   Did you see the football match last night?

V2   Yes, I did. You know, I couldn't understand the referee's decisions at all. He's usually so good. The team's behaviour was amazing considering all the mistakes the referee made. The manager's reaction wasn't as calm as it should've been.

V1   It was Alan White's first game as captain. A captain needs to be really tough and should be an excellent player. Captains need to set a good example too. The thing about him is he's so responsible. I liked the way he put a stop to the game when one of the other team's players got injured.

V2   Yes, he should definitely keep the job!

{ ping }

Now listen to the recording again.

CD2 Track 05

Question 4

(a)   **What does the air museum need money for the most?**

(b)   **What type of aircraft is new to the air museum?**

V1   One of the town's well-known tourist attractions is the air museum, with the largest collection of aircraft in the country. Although some money from the admission fees goes towards improving the facilities, and some on staff salaries, the vast majority of the profits are used for aircraft conservation before planes can be put on public display. An exhibition of historically important aircraft right at the entrance to the museum has recently been expanded. As well as the old passenger planes that have been there for a while, there are some rescue helicopters which have been added to the exhibition very recently.

{ ping }

Now listen to the recording again.

CD2 Track 06

Exercise 2

You will hear a talk given by a young man called Ray Cole, who cycled through seven countries in Central America. Listen to the talk and complete the sentences below. Write one or two words only in each gap.

You will hear the talk twice.

V1   My name's Ray Cole and last year I cycled through seven countries in Central America, including Mexico, Guatemala, Honduras and Costa Rica. Planning this trip was an enormous challenge. The budget was something I looked at carefully, though I was confident I wasn't going to spend too much once I'd paid for the flights. As for my language skills, I made sure I could manage a conversation in Spanish. My main concern was my fitness because I hadn't trained that much. Would I be able to cope?

This was the trip of a lifetime and I had about four months to do it. As for breaking records I just didn't care. It really wasn't about that. Going sightseeing isn't something cyclists always have the time to do, but I decided I'd take breaks to ensure I could explore the local culture.

On my trip I saw an incredible variety of different landscapes – including a mountain range called the Sierra Madre, and a beautiful hilly area which fortunately wasn't so tiring to cycle through! There was a jungle that I remember vividly, though it was a desert that left the biggest impression on me, but I didn't stay too long there!

I have to say that the heat was difficult to bear at times, especially when it was combined with high humidity. And yet it was the altitude that caught me out. I wasn't really prepared for it and it made me feel quite unwell. I often had to stop for a while to recover. Surprisingly, I faced a lot of strong wind at various times during the trip, though I was used to this from riding in other places.

I didn't particularly want to sleep outside or use campsites during this trip. But in many areas I struggled to find hostels where I could stay the night, and I was usually nowhere near towns with even small hotels. This meant I depended on local hospitality and when I was offered the chance to stay in people's homes, I was more than grateful.

Cycling for most of the day is obviously exhausting, so I had to keep my strength up the best I could. I ate bananas regularly while I was on the road, though I reckon I got most benefit from cereal bars. Jellied sweets are often recommended. However, things like that don't really appeal to me. In the evening, I'd eat a fair amount of potatoes and a great variety of beans were widely available.

The bike coped well with most conditions. The wheels weren't damaged by the rocky roads in some areas, and although the bike frame got battered it was more or less OK. I had a sophisticated GPS system which I thought might go wrong. In fact, it was reliable. A few days before reaching my final destination, my cooking equipment let me down, and I had to eat in local cafes.

When I got home, I regretted I hadn't filmed my trip and made a documentary about it. I thought about starting a travel website instead. It would have been a good way to educate people about the interesting places in Central America I'd visited. All I managed was a magazine article. I was quite proud of it actually.

© Cambridge University Press 2018

{ ping }

Now listen to the talk again.

CD2 Track 07

Exercise 3

You will hear six people talking about meals they have had. For each of Speakers 1 to 6, choose from the list, A to G, which opinion each speaker expresses. Write the letter in the appropriate box. Use each letter only once. There is one extra letter which you do not need to use.

You will hear the recordings twice.

Speaker 1

V1 I had a picnic in the park with my friends. It was a beautiful afternoon and we were supposed to be studying together in the library in town. We suddenly decided to have a picnic instead. We go to the park quite often, although it's small and often crowded. We hadn't thought things through in advance, so we ended up not buying enough stuff. A good picnic has different snacks for everyone to enjoy. Ours didn't quite match up to that. We'd have enjoyed it more if we'd cooked something too.

Speaker 2

V2 I had lunch at the top of a skyscraper. I was with my uncle who was going to introduce me to some of his business contacts, though they were too busy to make it. It was a spacious modern restaurant and it could take a large number of diners. It was very quiet at first, but bit by bit it got busier and things were quite lively. I couldn't believe the range of dishes. It was a pity the weather was so foggy that we didn't have a good view of the city.

Speaker 3

V3 My family prepared a meal to celebrate my grandmother's birthday. We discussed going to a famous restaurant next to a beautiful lake. However, in the end we organised a party at home. I've got a huge family and just about everyone turned up, including second or third cousins who I'd never actually met before, so that was exciting. Somehow we just about had room for everyone. The atmosphere was great and everyone was laughing and joking all night long. My parents cooked everything but stuck to a few basic dishes rather than doing too much fancy stuff.

Speaker 4

V4 When I was on holiday my mother took me to a restaurant in what was a very old building, though when I was inside I didn't see or feel the history. The restaurant had a great reputation, but the menu was limited and I was hoping for more choice. We met one of her Italian friends and I thought she might be a bit boring. Actually she was very entertaining and we got on well. It was busy and a bit noisy there, though that didn't spoil the atmosphere.

Speaker 5

V5 We had an end of term party at my college. The final year students were involved in planning the event and they were really enthusiastic. It could've been quite chaotic – just like last term, but the organisation was reasonably OK. Food wasn't the main focus of the evening, to be honest, so the ambitious plans for cooking lots of dishes got cut right back. At the start, the mood was very lively; then suddenly people started to feel sad because they realised they were leaving the school forever.

Speaker 6

V6 Last week I went to the official opening of a new restaurant in town. There were lots of important people there apparently, though they were all in their special VIP area. There were a lot of different dishes available, which is what you'd expect on an occasion like that. It was crowded and there wasn't enough room for some of the guests. All that could have changed the mood of the event, but the atmosphere was great throughout the evening.

{ ping }

Now listen to the six speakers again.

CD2 Track 08

Exercise 4

You will hear an interview with a woman called Isabelle Navarro, who manages rock bands. Listen to the interview and look at the questions. For each question, choose the correct answer, A, B or C, and put a tick in the appropriate box.

You will hear the interview twice.

V1 Today I'm talking to Isabelle Navarro who has managed three famous bands. Isabelle, how do you choose which group to manage?

V2 I take on bands which have had some success in their area, even if they're not nationally famous yet. The groups may have some practical business skills, though I don't think that's essential because I am better at helping people who don't have a clue about organising themselves. Confidence can help a new band, but it isn't sufficient on its own.

V1 Can you tell us something about when you took on your first ever band?

V2 I was still fairly young and at that stage I'd given up my dreams of becoming a pop star, but anyway an acquaintance who knew about my business degree and love of music asked me if I would like to manage a band. I don't think she realised how challenging such a job can be, while I was perfectly aware of the likely difficulties. However, I agreed and then started reading the biography of a famous manager. It made me think it wasn't the job for me!

V1 Was it a great feeling when your first band had their first number one record?

V2 The band got a lot of media attention but I wasn't interviewed, which suited me fine. The song was very original and my concern was that producing a second hit would be hard to achieve. Choosing to release such an unusual song had been mainly my decision, and I was convinced I was right, despite everyone doubting me.

V1 What do you think a new band should do in its first few months?

V2 Well, I'd say that bands shouldn't be in any hurry to get into the recording studio. Bands need time to find the right style, and that can't be done by getting the opinions of every musician they happen to know. It's natural for bands to look at what the current trends are. The problem is this can distract them from working out who they are and where their true talents lie.

V1 Tell me something about how you got on with the most famous band you managed, the Big Cats.

V2 When we met we hit it off immediately and I had very few doubts that we could work together. It all depended on being totally honest, and that often meant upsetting band members – at least for a while. If a song was not going to sell, I had to say so. These arguments made it hard to keep the partnership going for long, though it was never the plan to continue for more than a year.

V1 You usually manage bands that play soft rock, don't you?

V2 Yes, and everyone assumes that I don't understand other musical styles, which is unfair and not true. I appreciate a range of music, but my tastes have changed over the years, certainly compared to when I was young and into heavy metal! I only manage bands who play soft rock simply because I've done well with them and

they recommend me to other performers who are interested in the same sort of music.

V1 What kind of person do you have to be to succeed in your career?

V2 A good sense of humour helps because so much can go wrong in this business. The job involves a range of responsibilities – it's not just about money and contracts, it's about being creative, and looking after people. It's tough and often I'm up at five and in bed after midnight, though I'd say I do a better job when I relax regularly and avoid working round the clock.

V1 How has the music business changed recently?

V2 Well, some people say that increasingly bands don't hire managers, though others disagree. I've certainly noticed that nowadays musicians think they can become stars almost straight away; they're just not patient. Another change that we may see soon is bands talking to their fans more and the fans telling them what sort of direction they want the band to go in – that's interesting isn't it?

{ ping }

Now listen to the interview again.

CD2 Track 09

Exercise 5 part (a)

You will hear a talk by an oceanographer, a scientist who studies the sea. Listen to the talk and complete the notes in part (a). Write one or two words only.

You will hear the talk twice.

V1 My name's Oliver Connors and I work as an oceanographer. Scientists in my field study everything that is connected with the sea, including the underwater ecosystem. Oceanographers also examine the geology of the sea floor. My first year as an oceanographer was spent focusing on coastal erosion. I admit I preferred to be out at sea, and later I turned my attention to ocean currents and to dramatic events such as tidal waves.

What's fascinating about being an oceanographer is the range of projects that we participate in. Last year I had the opportunity to explore a volcano under the Pacific. I was busy with other work at the time, but six months later I jumped at the chance to do research on a shipwreck. It was about 400 years old and was lying at the bottom of the Baltic Sea, and it was certainly the highlight of my career so far.

Currently, I'm leading a team engaged in mapping the sea bed in detail, while searching for new species. I'm based at sea on a research

© Cambridge University Press 2018

ship called *Nereid*. Although we have a small submarine at our disposal that can carry three passengers, it's actually more effective to send down a robotic vehicle and so we've relied on nothing else.

The mission was proceeding in a fairly routine way when my team saw some unusual fish, which at first we thought were completely new. A careful check revealed that in fact they were rare but not unknown. Coming across some fossils which dated back 450 million years was a most unexpected event. The chances of finding something bigger like dinosaur bones are very remote though.

I believe my job is a vitally important one nowadays because there are a number of serious threats to the long-term health of the oceans. There is much discussion about the massive increase in the amount of carbon dioxide in the atmosphere. There is severe flooding in many parts of the globe, and the danger of islands disappearing. We shouldn't forget the fact that the presence of carbonic acid in the oceans may make it impossible for most species to survive in the long term, and there are emergencies such as oil spills that can be serious. But I'm particularly concerned about plastic pollution. There's so much of it in the ocean and it can have very harmful effects. Urgent action needs to be taken.

{ ping }

Now listen to the talk again.

CD2 Track 10

Exercise 5 part (b)

Now listen to a conversation between two students about exploring and protecting the oceans and complete the sentences in part (b). Write one or two words only, or a number, in each gap.

You will hear the conversation twice.

V1   The talk about oceanography was great, wasn't it? I couldn't believe how many weird types of marine animal there are, especially on the sea bed. I've found some images online. These squid are amazing creatures.

V2   For me, seahorses are the ones that just take my breath away.

V1   I know exactly what you mean. And look at the spiny crabs!

V2   They're not as fascinating, for me, as angler fish, which can produce light from antennae on their

heads to help them find their prey in the deep pitch-black sea they inhabit.

V1   There's certainly incredible biodiversity in the sea.

V2   I'm intrigued by exactly how deep you can go underwater. There's a place called the Mariana Trench which is 2500 kilometres long and 69 kilometres wide on average. When scientists first tried to measure the depth in 1875 they came up with a figure of 7 kilometres. Modern measurements are more accurate and show that the trench extends down as far as 11 kilometres. Bear in mind that the average depth of the ocean is 3.5 kilometres. I'd love to visit the Mariana Trench!

V1   I'm not sure I would. For a start the darkness down there must be quite scary. And I've read that at the bottom of the sea the temperatures are pretty much zero.

V2   I've heard that too, though I didn't have a clue about the pressure down there. Apparently it's about a thousand times greater than on the land!

V1   Wow, that's news to me. I've also read online that studying the ocean can lead to discoveries in several scientific areas. Oceanographers have found bacteria which produce valuable chemicals. Apparently, these can be used to treat some serious illnesses, so this could be extremely beneficial to medicine. There might be advances in physics – though I can't explain what they might be – and in meteorology too; both these areas seem less significant, however.

V2   I think you're right. And there are the environmental threats to consider. Some fish stocks are extremely low with a 90% reduction in some species in the last few years, and then there are the sharks, with millions killed annually, though I'm not sure what I can do about either problem. Volunteers can help prevent the destruction of coral reefs. If I could join a project with that aim it'd be absolutely brilliant!

V1   Yes, it would! Good luck with it!

{ ping }

Now listen to the conversation again.

Practice Test 4
CD2 Track 11

Exercise 1

You will hear four short recordings. Answer each question on the line provided. Write no more than three words for each answer.

You will hear each recording twice.

Question 1

(a) **Who has done something special at the school this year?**

(b) **What characteristic is most important for everyone at the school?**

V1 Boys and girls, it's been another successful year at Lakeside Secondary School. The builders have not quite finished our new science block, though we hope the official opening will be sometime in October. The volleyball team managed to win the regional cup despite having big problems at the start of the autumn term. Final year students are waiting for their academic results, which I'm very confident will match last year's achievements. I'd like to say that students should show determination as well as trying if at all possible to demonstrate skill and intelligence. But I should remind you that kindness to others is what matters above all.

{ ping }

Now listen to the recording again.

CD2 Track 12

Question 2

(a) **What did the girl find difficult about baking a cake?**

(b) **How does the girl describe the cake she made?**

V1 I can't believe you baked a cake!

V2 Well, things didn't quite go according to plan. I thought finding the ingredients would be challenging. In fact, I had some help with that. Following the recipe was OK, though I nearly missed one important step. It was bad time keeping that got me into trouble.

V1 But what about the final result?

V2 My father usually criticises my sister's cakes for being too dry. To be honest, I was more worried about the sugar and making my cake too sweet, but it wasn't a problem. I'd say it was too ambitious. Anyway, maybe next time I can make one for you!

{ ping }

Now listen to the recording again.

CD2 Track 13

Question 3

(a) **Which part of the new bike did the boy have a big problem with?**

(b) **Where does the boy regularly cycle to?**

V1 I love your new bike!

V2 I got it second-hand to save money. But I regret it now! I quickly realised the brakes weren't working properly. Getting that fixed cost a lot. My sister even said the handlebars weren't right. I couldn't see that myself. The gears aren't perfect but they'll do!

V1 Do you use your bike a lot?

V2 I'd like to take it along the river. Unfortunately, it's too muddy at this time of year. I mainly use my bike to get to the swimming pool. I train there five times a week. I'm not keen on the busy roads to the city centre so I only cycle there very occasionally.

{ ping }

Now listen to the recording again.

CD2 Track 14

Question 4

(a) **What does the woman think is the most impressive thing about a golden eagle?**

(b) **What is the main food eaten by golden eagles?**

V1 The golden eagle is a bird with enormous wings, which can be up to two metres long, though other birds of prey around the world are similar in size. Despite its name, it's dark brown with the golden colour concentrated around the neck and head, and not easily visible from a distance. What stands out for me is the fact it's capable of astonishing speed. It's interesting to watch it hunting. It takes a wide range of prey including fish and other birds. It has even been known to attack young deer. The largest part of its diet consists of rabbits. According to recent research, foxes are far less commonly eaten.

{ ping }

Now listen to the recording again.

CD2 Track 15

Exercise 2

You will hear a talk given by a young woman called Christina Lawson, who's taken up gardening as a new hobby. Listen to the talk and complete the sentences below. Write one or two words only in each gap.

You will hear the talk twice.

V1 I've recently taken up a new hobby – gardening. Although my father's a keen gardener, initially it didn't appeal to me. However, I'd always enjoyed eating strawberries fresh from the garden every summer, and thought the potatoes my father grew tasted better than anything from the supermarket! Anyway, I started experimenting by growing carrots which got eaten by snails, so I moved on to peas. I was pleased with the results and thought that maybe gardening was for me after all.

I can't deny that gardening involves hard work! Things like planting seeds are quite enjoyable. Watering plants is time-consuming but necessary. Other jobs like cutting the grass aren't that difficult with the right equipment. Digging isn't something most gardeners like doing and I'm no exception to the rule. But the work you do is worth it in the end.

There are many challenges. Various insects can attack your plants if you don't protect them: and there's the threat of disease too. I love birds but they cause problems by eating your fruit. I'm sorry to say that there's not much you can do about frost, especially if it comes at a time of year when you aren't expecting it. Unfortunately, I lost my favourite plants because of that last year.

There's a scientific side to gardening which I've just started getting into. I'm constantly learning new stuff. For example, how do you look after the soil so that the plants grow well? I was surprised to discover that kitchen waste helps. I don't believe you should use fertilisers or other chemicals. You can spread dead leaves on the soil, which I've tried several times, and old newspapers can be effective too.

One part of our garden was quite wild. I suggested having a pond there because it would make the garden more beautiful as well as attracting wildlife. My family wanted to have a picnic table, or even plant a cherry tree, so I gave up on my original idea.

At the bottom of the garden there used to be an old shed – you know, a place for storing tools and flowerpots. It was in such a bad condition we pulled it down. My first thought was to have a bench to sit on. Eventually we constructed something more ambitious, a greenhouse, which means we can grow plants requiring warmer conditions all the year round. A summer house would have been great, but the garden's not big enough!

Because most people love flowers, a friend tried without success to persuade me to have a rose garden. However, it's likely that part of the vegetable garden will be turned over to a different use. I'd love to set up a herb garden because I've become particularly interested in those plants recently. I appreciate what a difference they can make to my favourite dishes!

Now gardening is just a hobby, but I wondered about doing a job connected to it. Being a botanist is a possibility, but it's too challenging, and working as a soil scientist doesn't appeal much either. I'd really like to train to become a landscape gardener. Being a garden photographer would also be cool, but I'm not aiming for that.

{ ping }

Now listen to the talk again.

CD2 Track 16

Exercise 3

You will hear six people talking about their experiences of visiting famous tourist attractions. For each of Speakers 1 to 6, choose from the list, A to G, which opinion each speaker expresses. Write the letter in the appropriate box. Use each letter only once. There is one extra letter which you do not need to use.

You will hear the recordings twice.

Speaker 1

V1 I recently visited an interesting medieval town. It used to be hard to get to without a car, though fortunately a new train station has just opened. It's a small place so unless you want to explore every historic building, a few hours are sufficient to see the sights. The guidebooks don't prepare you for how wonderful the architecture is and don't rate the place highly, which is strange. Even so, it's full of tourists in the summer. I must have been lucky because it was fairly quiet the day I was there.

Speaker 2

V2 I visited an aquarium with hundreds of types of marine life. I'd been warned about the crowds and it was true, but I was so fascinated by the creatures I hardly noticed the other tourists. I was impressed by the aquarium cinema which showed films about underwater life and by the talks by experts about whales and dolphins. I visited every section and I didn't feel I had to rush. My friends had recommended the place and described it in detail and what they said turned out to be exactly right.

Speaker 3

V3 I went to a new art gallery. It's not right in the centre of town, though there are no problems accessing it by bus. Some paintings took my breath away and the modern art amazed me. The reviews include detailed descriptions so visitors know exactly what they're going to see, so they won't be surprised by anything, but neither will they be disappointed. The gallery was busy, though I was able to see everything clearly. It's not a big gallery and you can get round it fairly quickly, though I'd recommend taking your time.

Speaker 4

V4   I visited a national park last summer. I thought it might be in the middle of nowhere and hard to access. In fact, the roads are pretty good and it's clearly signposted. I'd read about it and it was more or less what I'd imagined. I was still disappointed by the number of visitors and the picnic area was very noisy. It's a huge park. I'm sure some visitors are disappointed they can't get to see all the different types of landscape there. I wasn't too ambitious and just spent my time in the forest.

Speaker 5

V5   At the weekend I visited a transport museum. Although it's a small museum, it's so fascinating I ended up spending much longer there than I intended – not that I regret it! The tickets are reasonably priced considering the quality of the exhibits. The facilities could do with some modernisation, though they're acceptable and I'd read the online reviews and knew that the strength of the museum was in its exhibits rather than things like the café and gift shop! Once the museum is better known it'll be busy. For now, it's a very pleasant day out.

Speaker 6

V6   I visited a shopping centre which attracts thousands of tourists. It's famous for the range of shops. I was determined to find some bargains. The reality is that the shops are all quite posh and mostly too expensive for me. I arrived early and had such a great time browsing in some of the clothes shops. I wanted to visit every floor, and had to spend the whole day there – I was exhausted at the end of it all! There were lots of people there. I guess that's normal in a shopping centre.

{ ping }

Now listen to the six speakers again.

CD2 Track 17

Exercise 4

You will hear an interview with a man called Alex Murray, an actor who works in the theatre. Listen to the interview and look at the questions. For each question,

choose the correct answer, A, B or C, and put a tick in the appropriate box.

You will hear the interview twice.

V1   With us today is the stage actor, Alex Murray. Welcome Alex. What's the best thing about acting on stage rather than being a TV actor?

V2   Well, it's quite stressful. I have to try and get everything right the first time. I can't stop and repeat a scene. I'm not sure whether this stress makes me a better actor! But it's thrilling having the audience there. I can feel their emotional reactions. When filming something for TV, I have no idea what people are going to think. Both types of work demand a lot and can be fulfilling, though.

V1   What do you remember about your first ever time acting on stage?

V2   It was with my school drama club. I had a minor role that nobody really noticed – but I had to start somewhere. A friend with a fairly important role was ill and I was asked to take his place. My friend couldn't understand why the teachers thought I should do it! Anyway, I reluctantly agreed, but was nervous and made several mistakes. Everyone was very understanding and my willingness to help in an emergency was appreciated. People ignored the fact I wasn't very good!

V1   How do you get a part in a play? You go to an audition, don't you?

V2   That's right. You act in a short scene in front of the director. Actors get used to attending auditions and it's just part of life so there's little point in me complaining. Sometimes I have to act alongside someone who isn't a professional actor, something I try to ignore. I don't know whether I've done well and am sometimes surprised to be offered work after what I thought was a fairly average audition.

V1   When you get a part in a play, what's the first thing you do?

V2   I know actors who watch videos of other professionals playing the part, and take notes. That might be useful. I prefer to think about the character and get a picture in my mind about what he's like. I do this by myself. There isn't usually enough time to discuss with colleagues how they will be tackling their parts.

V1   How hard it is to remember all your lines?

V2   I have a reasonably good memory, but even so, it tends to be a struggle, and most actors will tell you something similar. I get friends to help me as soon as I've got the script. Their support is not essential, though it can make the process more fun. Over the years I've found my brain works more effectively in the evenings so I tend to do most of my learning then.

V1   Do you get on well with the directors you work with?

V2   Every director has their individual style and methods. Some actors might be surprised, or even feel uneasy, when they meet a director with a new way of doing things. For me, it just makes life interesting. I try to be flexible and go with what the director requests because I don't like a tense atmosphere. A few directors discuss all aspects of the play and every line. It's like being in a classroom! That kind of analysis does help actors though.

V1   I guess wearing the costume for the first time is an important moment.

V2   I'm sometimes shocked when I see the costume because it's not how I imagined my character looking. However, I avoid complaining and demanding a different costume. And the other thing is that I've decided by then how I'm going to play the part and there's no way I can reconsider. Wearing that costume makes me tense, though. I realise I'll soon be on the stage in front of the audience.

V1   What do you think of the journalists who write reviews of your plays?

V2   Many actors are upset when they read criticism, despite the fact that most reviews are fair and balanced. Others really dislike the journalists, though they're just doing their jobs in my opinion. The journalists are experts so it's not as if they don't know what they're talking about. Sometimes they even make interesting points that I can benefit from.

{ ping }

Now listen to the interview again.

CD2 Track 18

Exercise 5 part (a)

You will hear a teacher giving a talk about the history of toys. Listen to the talk and complete the notes in part (a). Write one or two words only.

You will hear the talk twice.

V1   Before we visit the museum to see a wide range of toys from many historical periods, I'm going to say something about the history of toys.

Astonishingly, wax dolls have been found that are 4000 years old, and clay animals were toys in India at around the same time. In China children played with kites at least 2000 years ago. Some rather sophisticated toys have a surprisingly long history, for example, the first mechanical puzzles, which were known to have existed in Greece 2300 years ago.

In eighteenth-century Europe there was a significant increase in the number and variety of toys that were available. Some were designed to help children acquire practical skills, such as rocking horses. Other children received puppet theatres as presents, though these sometimes presented a challenge as they had to assemble them! Toys increasingly had a clear educational purpose. The first board games were developed in the 1750s aimed at teaching children something about different countries. Toy soldiers became more popular around this time too, though these presumably weren't intended to educate children.

In the 19th century, dolls houses were sold in large numbers. These houses looked quite realistic and had lots of beautiful detail in them. It's fascinating to study the tiny items that children could play with in these houses. Of course, the houses contained toy furniture. But there was also toy fruit, and toy meat, both of which children could use as part of their games. There was even toy medicine. I was really impressed by that.

In the early 1900s toy manufacturers tried to appeal to creative children who liked to work with their hands. Toys were developed that were based on ideas used in engineering. Suddenly, these so-called construction sets became a hit with children everywhere. These were much more complex than the wooden blocks sold previously, and gave children the opportunity to design and make model trains, or later on, spaceships.

Television and cinema has had a considerable impact on children's culture. In the early years of the cinema cartoon characters weren't necessarily made into toys, and at this point superheroes remained in comics rather than films. However, nowadays the large number of action figures in the shops proves that toys are increasingly used to promote TV shows or films. More innocent things like stuffed animals belonged to a less commercial age.

{ ping }

Now listen to the talk again.

CD2 Track 19

Exercise 5 part (b)

Now listen to a conversation between two students about their visit to the toy museum and complete the sentences in Part (b). Write one or two words only in each gap.

You will hear the conversation twice.

V1 The visit to the museum was really fun. Many toys have such a long history. I knew skipping ropes were quite recent and I'm not sure about hoops, though kids definitely used them in the 19th century. The astonishing thing is that chess dates back 1500 years.

V2 That was news to me too. I liked the spinning tops. Apparently they were popular in the second half of the 19th century.

V1 We're so used to seeing plastic toys. But toys can be made from almost anything.

V2 Yes, the bronze elephants from India we saw were awesome. I spent a while examining the dominoes closely because I used to play that game. They were carved from wood and looked great. I liked the metal trains too, and some dolls made from card. It was a cheap material but they were still impressive.

V1 My favourite toys were inspired either by science-fiction or science-fact.

V2 Yes, in 1969 Neil Armstrong walked on the surface of the Moon. The toys reflected that important event, I guess.

V1 That's right. There was a wonderful space rocket on display. It was a really detailed model. That must have been so exciting – better than the model aircraft most kids were into before that. The big Hollywood sci-fi films also inspired different types of toy robot too.

V2 The next section was best – the one about electronic toys. There was a virtual pet toy and other fun things.

V1 Apparently, the first electronic toys came out in 1976. The Little Professor was the name of quite a serious toy, which gave children a number and they had to work out how to get that number by doing calculations. There was something called the Auto Race too, released in the same year. It only used about 500 bytes of memory – amazing when compared to games today!

V2 I liked the look of Merlin, the electronic wizard. It consisted of six games on one device, including something called the Music Machine game, which was quite popular. That one came out around 1980, I think.

V1 The guide told us about the importance of innovation for toy manufacturers. She didn't cover prices, which is what matters to parents! The stuff on safety regulations was a waste of time, even though I know they are important.

V2 Yes, it was a boring way to end the tour. The bit about recycling toys was OK. We could even use it in our environmental studies project!

{ ping }

Now listen to the conversation again.

© Cambridge University Press 2018

Acknowledgements

The authors and publishers acknowledge the following sources of copyright material and are grateful for the permissions granted. While every effort has been made, it has not always been possible to identify the sources of all the material used, or to trace all copyright holders. If any omissions are brought to our notice, we will be happy to include the appropriate acknowledgements on reprinting.

Test 2 R&W Ex. 1 adapted from '14 years old and worth £2m: meet Norfolk's 'mini Monet' by Charlotte Lytton, Telegraph, 9 September 2016 © Telegraph Media Group Limited 2016

Thanks to the following for permission to reproduce images:

Cover Daniel A. Leifheit/Getty Images

Inside in order of appearance Westend61/Getty Images; Blend Images- KidStock/Brand X Pictures/Getty Images; drferry/iStock/Getty Images; Tsidvintsev/iStock/Getty Images; Krasyuk/iStock/Getty Images; Washington Imaging/Alamy Stock Photo; James Porcini/Cultura/Getty Images; Onne van der Wal/Corbis Documentary/Getty Images; Thomas Kitchin & Victoria Hurst/All Canada Photos/Getty Images; Mitchell Krog/Getty Images; Matthew Micah Wright/Lonely Planet Images/Getty Images; coberschneider/RooM/Getty Images; Geber86/E+/Getty Images; Ryan McVay/Stone/Getty Images; DANIEL GARCIA/AFP/Getty Images; AndreyPopov/iStock/Getty Images; Stringer/Anadolu Agency/Getty Images; nicolamargaret/E+/Getty Images; Dougal Waters/DigitalVision/Getty Images; swissmediavision/E+/Getty Images

BLANK PAGE

Answer key
Practice Test 1
Reading and Writing

Exercise 1

Question	Answer	Marks
1	Li taught herself	1
2	(the) bank	1
3	cooking for a top hotel	1
4	calm	1
5	her warm character AND her creative approach ONE MARK for each	2
6	her husband	1
7	she put on weight / she put on (over) 5 kilos	1
8	(her) diary	1
9	1 mark for each detail up to a maximum of 4 marks: • move to London (in the next few months) • opening own café (later this year) • supply (some well-known) restaurants with (her) recipes • launch a cookery school (next year) • start filming a documentary series (about spices)	4

Exercise 2

Question	Answer	Marks
10(a)	D	1
10(b)	B	1
10(c)	A	1
10(d)	C	1
10(e)	B	1
10(f)	A	1
10(g)	C	1
10(h)	A	1
10(i)	D	1
10(j)	B	1

Exercise 3

Question	Answer	Marks
11	1 mark for each acceptable response, up to a maximum of 3 marks: • advising makers of TV documentaries (on the subject of dinosaurs) • teaching • (coming up with) new research projects	3
12	1 mark for each acceptable response, up to a maximum of 3 marks: • move (much) faster • a lot more intelligent • darker / less colourful • featherless	3
13	1 mark for each acceptable response, up to a maximum of 3 marks: • what caused the dinosaurs to disappear • how they interacted (with each other) • what sounds dinosaurs (might have) made • how dinosaurs (originally) developed	3

Exercise 4

Question	Answer	Marks
14	Relevant points to include: • (makes) children happier • perform difficult tasks better • develop social skills • learn to speak faster • good at learning other languages • ability to deal with numbers improves / good at maths • (develop) good physical co-ordination / move in a smooth and efficient way • improves memory • (improves) ability to concentrate • achieve higher scores in various school subjects • (greater) self-confidence	8

© Cambridge University Press 2018

Exercise 5

Sample answer A

> Hi Jackie
>
> I hope you're well.
>
> I think I told you my school has a new music centre. It has four rooms for playing and recording music in. It's really cool. Our headteacher asked some students <u>helping</u> organise a party to celebrate the new centre, and I was one of the students he asked.
>
> We organised a party for the whole school, with families welcome too. That's a lot of people! It was on the first Sunday in May from 2–9pm, and we had to arrange food, drinks, live music and other entertainment. Me and two other students were responsible <u>to</u> the publicity. As well as posting lots of messages about it on the school website and on social media, we put posters up around the school.
>
> The party was very <u>success</u>. I think it's really important <u>events like this</u>. When you have fun together, you feel more positive about your school, and that has a good impact on your studies. Also, it was an opportunity for some students to play music in public, and some of them were surprisingly good.
>
> I must stop now, but I'll write again soon.
>
> Take care.
>
> Leila

(193 words)

Comments

Content: All three points are covered in some detail. The style is appropriate and the writer is very clear about why she is writing and who she is writing to. The content is well-developed and of an appropriate length. The message is communicated skilfully and effectively throughout.

Language: There is a good range of common vocabulary used appropriately, and some less common words. Simple structures are used effectively, and a few more complex structures are used. The language is mostly very accurate, and the occasional errors do not impede understanding. The text is well-organised with good paragraphing and effective linking between sentences.

Marks: Content 8
        Language 7

Sample answer B

> Hi Jonny
>
> How are you?
>
> I recently helped to organise a special celebration in my school. It was a party <u>for finish</u> the school year. Everybody from my class and my year <u>is</u> invited. Their friends too. So

> everybody <u>is</u> 15 or 16 or 17 years old. We <u>have</u> the party in the school hall. It's a big room and perfect for parties. Me and Sara <u>prepare</u> a <u>lot</u> food like <u>sandwich</u> and pizza. Other students brought drinks and cakes. Also, I helped prepare the hall for dancing. My friend Jose <u>is</u> the DJ. He had a special music system and he <u>arrange</u> a cool selection of music for <u>dance</u> at the party. A <u>lot</u> people helped to prepare the party. Some teachers helped too and they were present <u>for check</u> all was OK. There was no problems and it was one of the best parties <u>I go</u> to <u>in all my life</u>.
>
> Sorry you couldn't come to the party.
>
> See you soon.
>
> Carmen

(164 words)

Comments

Content: The task is only partially fulfilled because the third point about why it's important for schools to organise celebrations is not covered. However, the first two points are covered in some detail, the style is appropriate and it is clear who the writer is writing to and why she is writing. Despite language errors, the content is clearly communicated.

Language: Common vocabulary is used appropriately. The structures used are mainly simple with few attempts at more complex structures. There are errors in most sentences including the use of verb forms, prepositions, verb tenses and singular/plural. However, the errors do not prevent the meaning from coming through. The text is reasonably well organised, with the sequence of information clear and some linking words used. However, more effective paragraphing would make the text easier to read.

Marks: Content 4
        Language 4

Exercise 6

Sample answer A

> Christopher Boone, the main character in 'The Curious Incident of the Dog in the Night-Time', is a teenager with an extremely logical brain and an amazing talent for maths and remembering huge quantities of facts. He also likes animals, but he hates the colours yellow and brown, and he doesn't much like meeting people because he doesn't understand their emotions.
>
> Christopher uses his talents to investigate the death of a dog, so it's a strange kind of detective story. What makes it special is that Christopher has a disability called Asperger's syndrome, and the author tells the story from his point of view. We see everything through Christopher's eyes, <u>that's</u> a fascinating way to see things.

> Some parts of the story are very sad, even shocking – it can be upsetting to see the world through the eyes of someone who <u>don't</u> have 'normal' feelings. Some parts of it, however, are very funny. It touches you on a deep emotional level, but it also makes you realise that not everybody sees the world in the same way <u>of</u> you. I think it is very important for young people to be aware of this.

(192 words)

Comments

Content: The student fulfils the task well. There is a well-developed explanation of what the book is about and a justification for recommending it to other young people. The style is appropriate and the purpose of the review is clear. The length is appropriate, and the information is communicated skilfully and effectively.

Language: A wide range of common and less common vocabulary is used effectively. Simple and more complex structures are also used well. The language is mostly very accurate, with just a few minor errors which do not affect understanding. The text is well-organised with good paragraphing and effective linking.

Marks: Content 8
Language 8

Sample answer B

> I love <u>watch</u> movies. I have one book <u>'The Film Book'</u> I <u>like it</u> very much. This book <u>tell</u> about 100 great movies. <u>Begin</u> with silent movies in about 1910 and <u>finished</u> in year 2010. In each movie it <u>tell</u> about <u>story, actors, how made</u>, and <u>why is it</u> a great film. In addition it <u>tell</u> about time in history when the film <u>is</u> made. You can learn a lot from movies about people, <u>lifestyle, thinking, feelings</u>. It <u>have</u> nice photographs and <u>easy</u> to read. My father is <u>movie</u> fan too. Sometimes we choose a film and read everything about it. Then we get the film from a website and we watch and we discuss the film. My dad and me <u>enjoy</u>. <u>Some my</u> friends only like new movies but <u>two my friends the</u> same <u>like</u> me. They like this book too.

(142 words)

Comments

Content: The student fulfils part of the task. There are some details on what the book is about and why the writer likes it. There is some reference to other young people but no clear explanation about why they should read it. There is no single format or writing style appropriate for reviews – they can be written in many different ways – and the style is reasonably appropriate here. At 142 words, it is slightly under the required length. In writing a short text, the writer misses the opportunity to demonstrate knowledge of a wider range of language.

Language: Common vocabulary is used appropriately. The structures used are mainly simple and sentences are generally short. There are errors in most sentences including the use of verb forms, articles, word order and the omission of words. The errors do not prevent the meaning from coming through, although they may get in the way of fluent reading. The text is reasonably well organised, with the sequence of information clear and some linking words used. However, the use of paragraphs would make the text more accessible.

Marks: Content 4
Language 3

Practice Test 1

Listening

Exercise 1

Question	Answer	Marks
1(a)	(a) (new/bigger/better) cupboard	1
1(b)	paint/decorate/redo (the/my/her) walls	1
2(a)	(the) weather	1
2(b)	eating more pasta	1
3(a)	(the) different styles	1
3(b)	(the) sound (quality)	1
4(a)	buying food	1
4(b)	(seeing) (old) friends	1

Exercise 2

Question	Answer	Marks
5(i)	watching whales	1
5(ii)	diving	1
5(iii)	walking shoes	1
5(iv)	cowboy film	1
5(v)	age	1
5(vi)	(natural) sunblock	1
5(vii)	kangaroo rat	1
5(viii)	rock paintings	1

Exercise 3

Question	Answer	Marks
6(i)	D	1
6(ii)	E	1
6(iii)	G	1
6(iv)	C	1
6(v)	F	1
6(vi)	A	1

Exercise 4

Question	Answer	Marks
7(a)	A	1
7(b)	B	1
7(c)	A	1
7(d)	B	1
7(e)	C	1
7(f)	A	1
7(g)	C	1
7(h)	B	1

Exercise 5

Question	Answer	Marks
8(a)(i)	minor planets	1
8(a)(ii)	irregular	1
8(a)(iii)	moons	1
8(a)(iv)	grey	1
8(a)(v)	celebrities	1
8(b)(i)	30/thirty metres/meters/m	1
8(b)(ii)	Telescopes	1
8(b)(iii)	rock samples / rocks / samples	1
8(b)(iv)	rare metals	1
8(b)(v)	rocket fuel	1

Practice Test 2
Reading and Writing
Exercise 1

Question	Answer	Marks
1	six/6	1
2	amazed	1
3	countryside (scenes)	1
4	determination	1
5	leaves the picture for a day	1
6	to protect their privacy	1
7	(joking around with) friends	1
8	learn from each other (in art groups) AND paint outside ONE MARK for each	2
9	1 mark for each detail up to a maximum of 4 marks: • playing football • cycling • listening to music • observing animals	4

Exercise 2

Question	Answer	Marks
10(a)	C	1
10(b)	A	1
10(c)	B	1
10(d)	D	1
10(e)	B	1
10(f)	A	1
10(g)	D	1
10(h)	B	1
10(i)	C	1
10(j)	A	1

Exercise 3

Question	Answer	Marks
11	1 mark for each acceptable response, up to a maximum of 3 marks: • (bits of) paint • (old) batteries • (unused) fuel • a tool	3
12	1 mark for each acceptable response, up to a maximum of 3 marks: • (a very expensive piece of) technology could be destroyed • (some) sections of space may (eventually) become unusable • human life may be at risk	3
13	1 mark for each acceptable response, up to a maximum of 3 marks: • space garbage trucks • international agreements (about dealing with man-made objects in space) • when a satellite becomes out-of-date, it should automatically return to earth • laser beams • a giant net	3

Exercise 4

Question	Answer	Marks
14	Relevant points to include: • tell yourself you can do it • work out short-term goals that you can achieve • consider how you will deal with difficult situations • work out how to block pain • focus on the money you will raise (for charity) • make yourself look up and around you (as you run) • think about the respect you will gain from others • take pride in all the running you've already done • remember that it will be very good for your health • don't forget to enjoy yourself	8

Exercise 5

Sample answer A

Hi Daniela

I want to tell you about a trip that my class went on last week to the Museum of Local History in the city centre. I think it's been there a long time but I never was there before.

As you know, I'm really interested in history, especially ancient history, and I was fascinated by all the objects that are two or three thousand years old there. For example, you can see tools that people used to make house, and some jewellery made from metal, shells and pieces of bone. You can read lots of information about everything too.

Half of the museum is about modern history, and, to be honest, I think some of that is a little boring. Some of my classmates did too. We didn't have a guide and I think that wasn't good. If we had a guide explaining things to us in a funny way, the modern history part of the museum was more interesting.

We also visited the museum shop and the café. They were OK but quite expensive. If the shop and the café was better I think more young people want to return to the museum.

See you soon.

Anne

(200 words)

Comments

Content: All three points are covered so the task is fulfilled. The style is appropriate and the writer is very clear about why she is writing and who she is writing to. The content is well-developed and of an appropriate length. The message is generally communicated skilfully and effectively.

Language: There is a good range of common vocabulary used appropriately. Simple structures are used effectively, and a few more complex structures are used, although these are not always used accurately. The language is mostly accurate, however, and errors do not impede communication. The text is well-organised with good paragraphing and effective linking between sentences.

Marks: Content 7
      Language 7

Sample answer B

Hi Gerry

I hope you're well.

I would like talk you about my class visit to museum. We went science museum. We went in bus with two teachers. There's very old building with 3 floors and 12 rooms.

Science is not my favourite but I like this museum. It teach you many things about science like human body, medicine, computers.

We stay there the all day but I can go again if you want go with me. The ticket for enter the museum is very cheap. I know you like science. They give many information about the world, the planets, the sun, the moon and you can look in telescopio and microscopio. One section of the museum is cars. Cars for me very interesting. The museum it have lots old cars and show how cars change. You can sit in some old cars but you can't drive them. It's a pity but I understand.

Well, Gerry. Can you write me soon?

Bye

Jonas

(163 words)

Comments

Content: The task is only partially fulfilled because the third point about how the museum could become more attractive to young people is not covered. However, the first two points are covered in some detail, the style is appropriate and it is clear who the writer is writing to and why he is writing. Despite language errors, the meaning is usually clear.

Language: Some common vocabulary is used appropriately. The structures used are mainly simple with a few compound sentences. There are errors in many sentences including the use of verb forms, prepositions, verb tenses and articles. The text is reasonably well organised, with the sequence of information clear, although there is little evidence of ability to use linking words.

Marks: Content 4
　　　 Language 3

Exercise 6

Sample answer A

Introduction

My geography teacher Mrs Hassan has asked students to write a report on an environmental issue in the school and to suggest improvements to the situation.

The issue

I have had discussions with several students and we all think that the school could be much better in terms of its energy use.

Firstly, a huge amount electrical power is wasted. Lights, computer equipment and air-conditioning units are left on in rooms when is there no-one. This is a waste of

money as well as energy. I have no information about the school's energy costs, but I am confident that they could be reduced.

Secondly, all the school's electricity comes from the national grid, which is power by oil and gas. It seems strange that we do not use sustainable energy in an area where we have a lot of sun and wind.

Suggestions

Firstly, the school should have a strict policy that lights, air-conditioning units and electrical equipment should always be switched off unless they are absolutely necessary. The school management should promote this policy but everyone in the school should play their roles.

Secondly, the possibility of installing solar panels and wind turbines so that the school generates its own electricity should be investigated. Financial support for introducing solar and wind power technology is available. In my view, there would be great benefits in making the school more environment-friendly.

(231 words)

Comments

Content: The task is fulfilled well. The style is consistently appropriate, the purpose of the report is clear and the audience is clearly indicated. There is a well-developed explanation of the environmental issue in the school and of the steps the school should take. The report is a little over-length (231 words), but the information is communicated skilfully and effectively.

Language: A wide range of common and less common vocabulary is used effectively. Simple and more complex structures are also used well. The language is mostly very accurate, with just a few minor errors which do not affect understanding. The text is well-organised in an appropriate report format, and there is effective linking.

Marks: Content 8
　　　 Language 8

Sample answer B

The environmental issue I choose is the litter. Too many students are very dirty. They put papers and plastic bottles and drinks cans in the classrooms, in the corredors, in the playgrounds, on the grass. It's horrible. Even they put chewing gum on the tables in the classrooms and on the floor. I don't understand this because there are plenty rubbish bins. Do they same in their houses? Maybe, maybe not. Maybe their mums clean everything. But they must to be more responsible. The school have people who clean but we mustn't make their job impossible.

The teachers should be very strict with the dirty students. For example, they can make them go to school at the weekend and clean everything. I think this is a good idea. Or if the teachers see a student drop litter, this student <u>must pay something</u>. <u>At the end the year</u>, all the money from this can pay for something new in the school. <u>They don't make litter again.</u>

(165 words)

Comments

Content: The task is generally fulfilled. The student identifies an environmental problem (litter), describes it and suggests solutions. The style is rather informal and inappropriate for a report. It is not clear who the report is for, but there is a sense of purpose. There is some development of content.

Language: Common vocabulary is used, mostly appropriately, although there are instances where the style is inconsistent and too informal. The structures used are mainly simple and sentences are often very short. There are numerous errors including the use of verb forms, articles, word order and prepositions. However, the errors do not prevent the meaning from coming through. The text is organised in two clear paragraphs, with the sequence of information clear and some linking words used. There is no single correct format for a report, but sub-headings would help the reader navigate the text.

Marks: Content 3
Language 4

Practice Test 2

Listening

Exercise 1

Question	Answer	Marks
1(a)	fashion	1
1(b)	finding new ideas	1
2(a)	(a/his) cat	1
2(b)	(very) professional	1
3(a)	(the/its) history	1
3(b)	honey	1
4(a)	(two) T-shirts	1
4(b)	(the) (loud) music	1

Exercise 2

Question	Answer	Marks
5(i)	June	1
5(ii)	rock concert	1
5(iii)	city gate	1
5(iv)	drummers	1
5(v)	film characters	1
5(vi)	Mexican	1
5(vii)	mini(-)golf	1
5(viii)	(some) fireworks	1

Exercise 3

Question	Answer	Marks
6(i)	G	1
6(ii)	F	1
6(iii)	A	1
6(iv)	D	1
6(v)	B	1
6(vi)	C	1

Exercise 4

Question	Answer	Marks
7(a)	A	1
7(b)	C	1
7(c)	B	1
7(d)	A	1
7(e)	B	1
7(f)	C	1
7(g)	C	1
7(h)	A	1

Exercise 5

Question	Answer	Marks
8(a)(i)	humidity	1
8(a)(ii)	examining	1
8(a)(iii)	banana plants	1
8(a)(iv)	(sound) vibrations	1
8(a)(v)	(educational) leaflets	1
8(b)(i)	habitat loss	1
8(b)(ii)	shelter	1
8(b)(iii)	(ripe) pears	1
8(b)(iv)	pesticides	1
8(b)(v)	Orange Tip / orange tip	1

Exercise 2

Question	Answer	Marks
9(a)	B	1
9(b)	D	1
9(c)	C	1
9(d)	A	1
9(e)	B	1
9(f)	C	1
9(g)	A	1
9(h)	D	1
9(i)	B	1
9(j)	A	1

Practice Test 3

Reading and Writing

Exercise 1

Question	Answer	Marks
1	(the) treks tend to be shorter (than those in Uganda)	1
2	July and August	1
3	to protect (the) gorillas	1
4	(she) had flu	1
5	one/1 hour	1
6	(have) longer fur AND (tend to be) larger ONE MARK for each	2
7	keep still AND avoid eye contact ONE MARK for each	2
8	1 mark for each detail up to a maximum of 4 marks: • waterproof clothes • waterproof bags (to protect camera equipment) • (gardening) gloves • long-sleeved tops • (strong) walking boots • (good pair of) binoculars	4

Exercise 3

Question	Answer	Marks
10	1 mark for each acceptable response, up to a maximum of 3 marks: • living and working by the sea • the opportunity to meet a (wide) variety of people • seeing a student managing to ride a wave	3
11	1 mark for each acceptable response, up to a maximum of 3 marks: • you earn very little money • you don't have much time to surf yourself • telling students that they can't go into the water • fixing the surfboards (when they get damaged)	3
12	1 mark for each acceptable response, up to a maximum of 3 marks: • passionate about surfing • (very) aware of safety • (a) good communicator • (very) fit	3

Exercise 4

Question	Answer	Marks
13	Relevant points to include: **Advantages of flying cars**: • would be able to move (much) faster (than normal cars) • could go straight from A to B • could (be used to) avoid traffic jams • don't require road systems (which are expensive to build and maintain) **Disadvantages of flying cars**: • safety is (still) a big issue / it's unclear what would happen if something went wrong • bad weather conditions (are a serious concern) / (up in the air) (the) wind is much stronger • setting up an air traffic control system for them (would be a huge challenge) • no-one knows what skills and permits people will need • places to take off from and land on will be needed • the cost will prevent most people from owning them / several times more expensive than a standard car	8

Exercise 5

Sample answer A

Hi John

I want tell you about problem with my teacher. She's name Maria Carson. She is my science teacher. She don't like me. I don't know why. She never give me good marks. Yesterday she say I'm bad student. I always do my homework but she tell I'm lazy boy. I always try speak with her. I ask why she don't think my work is good. What I do wrong? I don't understand her advice. It is confusion. John my friend can you give me advice? What I can do?

Best regards

Your friend Selim

(96 words)

Comments

Content: The task is only partially fulfilled because only one point (the problem) is clearly covered. The second

and third points are only indirectly referred to at best. The style is appropriate for a friend and it is clear who the writer is writing to and why. However, the candidate appears to have misunderstood the task. The meaning is usually clear but there is some repetition and the development of the content is limited. At 95 words, the email is much shorter than required.

Language: Some common vocabulary is used appropriately but the range of vocabulary is limited. The structures used are simple with only one more complex sentence. There are many grammatical errors, including the use of verb tenses and forms, singular/plural agreement, word order in questions and missing articles. There are no linking words so the text doesn't flow at all, and there is no attempt at paragraphing. The meaning is usually clear but control of language and organisation is limited.

Marks: Content 2
Language 2

Sample answer B

Hi Claire

I would like to tell you about one thing has happened last week with my teacher. I have been worried because my school work not has been very good. I don't know to write very good essay. Mr Bruno is very kind and he spoke with me a lot and he gave me lots of advices.

First, he said I must plan my writting more carful. I think this is essential. Second, Mr Bruno say I need write the essay and I must follow the plan when I write. Third point, I must leave the essay for few hours. I must do something different like sport. Then after some hours I have to return to the essay and read it again very carful. I have to correct the mistakes and change some things. Maybe I have some new ideas or more adequate words. It is a little boring to read the essay again but I know it is good idea.

Now I am doing my teachers advices and my writting is a little better. So tomorrow I want to say thank you my teacher very much.

OK Claire.

See you soon

Enrico

(194 words)

Comments

Content: All three points are clearly covered so the task is fulfilled. The style is mostly appropriate, although it seems too formal in places. The writer is clear about why he is writing and who he is writing to. The content is developed and of an appropriate length. The message is generally communicated effectively.

Language: There is a good range of common vocabulary used appropriately. Simple structures are used effectively, and there are a number of more complex sentences, but there is very little evidence of an ability to use more complex structures. The meaning is always clear but there are frequent language errors: verb tenses and forms, missing articles, adverb formation, singular/plural nouns, misspellings. The text is well-organised with effective paragraphing and linking between sentences.

Marks: Content 6
      Language 4

Exercise 6

Sample answer A

Chinese New Year is one of the most wide celebrated festivals in the world. Wherever there is a Chinese community, Chinese New Year is celebrated. In Singapore, 75% of the population is ethnic Chinese, so it's a big event here. In fact, it's a public holiday.

The first day of the festival falls on the new moon between 21st January and 20th February. On New Year's Eve we clean our houses to get rid of the bad luck from the previous year and clear the way for good luck then in the evening we have a big family dinner with lots of traditional Chinese food like dumplings and pineapple tart.

There are various other traditions along the festival. For example, young men like to set off firecrackers and other fireworks. We have street parades through the town, and adults put money in red envelopes and give them to children and teenagers, which is one tradition young people definitely look forward to!

The most important thing about the occasion is that it reminds us of our culture and our history, and it's a way of honouring our ancestors and families.

(189 words)

Comments

Content: The task is fulfilled well. The style is consistently appropriate, and there is an adequate sense of purpose and audience. The description of the festival is well-developed and there is an explanation of why the festival is important. The length is appropriate and the content is communicated skilfully and effectively.

Language: A wide range of common and less common vocabulary is used effectively. Some simple structures and a few more complex structures are used. The language is mostly accurate, with just a few minor errors which do not affect understanding. The text is well-organised, and there is effective linking.

Marks: Content 8
      Language 8

Sample answer B

If you want to see a fantastic festival, you must to come to Brazil in February for our carnival. The celebrations most famous are in Rio de Janeiro and Sao Paulo in the south and Salvador and Recife in the north-east of the country. Basically, carnival is an enormous six-day street party with music, dancing, singing, and eating. The carnival festivities come from Africa originally and it is still a strong African influence, but also carnival change with the time. In Rio and Sao Paulo, the typical carnival music is samba. Have huge organised parades of samba schools with thousands people dressed in costumes amazing and dancing through the streets. In the north-east, the popular musics are frevo and axe and the dancing is different. Also in the north east, the celebrations are more informal and less organised. Everybody mixes during carnival: young people, middle-aged, old, rich, middle-class and poor, and everyone have a great time. Brazilians know how to enjoy and carnival is when they enjoy themselves most. It is important because it's the occasion when everyone can forget their problems and just have fun. You must to come to carnival in Brazil one time in your life.

(199 words)

Comments

Content: The task is fulfilled. The festival is described with some development and detail and the importance of carnival is explained. The style is appropriate for an article of this kind and there is some sense of purpose and audience. The length is appropriate and the content is communicated effectively.

Language: Common vocabulary is used, mostly appropriately, and some less common vocabulary is used. A good range of simple structures is used appropriately, with a few examples of more complex structures. There are some errors including word order, problems with *there/it*, correct use of *must*, and singular/plural agreement. However, the meaning is always clear despite the errors. The text is coherent and some linking words are used. However, the article would be more accessible if it was divided into paragraphs.

Marks: Content 7
      Language 6

Practice Test 3

Listening

Exercise 1

Question	Answer	Marks
1(a)	(the) sports centre	1
1(b)	cheap tickets	1
2(a)	(the) North Pole / (the) north pole	1
2(b)	(the) amusing script	1
3(a)	(the) team's behaviour	1
3(b)	(he's) (so) responsible	1
4(a)	(aircraft) conservation	1
4(b)	rescue helicopters	1

Exercise 2

Question	Answer	Marks
5(i)	fitness	1
5(ii)	breaking records	1
5(iii)	desert	1
5(iv)	altitude	1
5(v)	people's homes	1
5(vi)	cereal bars	1
5(vii)	cooking equipment	1
5(viii)	magazine article	1

Exercise 3

Question	Answer	Marks
6(i)	B	1
6(ii)	A	1
6(iii)	D	1
6(iv)	G	1
6(v)	E	1
6(vi)	F	1

Exercise 4

Question	Answer	Marks
7(a)	B	1
7(b)	A	1
7(c)	B	1
7(d)	C	1
7(e)	A	1
7(f)	A	1
7(g)	C	1
7(h)	B	1

Exercise 5

Question	Answer	Marks
8(a)(i)	coastal erosion	1
8(a)(ii)	shipwreck / ship-wreck / ship wreck	1
8(a)(iii)	robotic vehicle	1
8(a)(iv)	fossils	1
8(a)(v)	plastic pollution	1
8(b)(i)	seahorses / sea-horses / sea horses	1
8(b)(ii)	eleven / 11	1
8(b)(iii)	pressure	1
8(b)(iv)	medicine	1
8(b)(v)	coral reefs	1

Practice Test 4

Reading and Writing

Exercise 1

Question	Answer	Marks
1	(a) sandstorm / (a) sand storm	1
2	(a) plastic palm tree	1
3	it's (a thousand metres/over 1000 m) higher AND (the) weather is (definitely) more extreme ONE MARK for each	2
4	she is a doctor	1
5	(by) collecting snow (to melt for tea)	1
6	built walls (of rocks around them)	1

© Cambridge University Press 2018

Question	Answer	Marks
7	the path's easier to walk on (if there's snow)	1
8	nine hours / 9 hours	1
9	1 mark for each detail up to a maximum of 4 marks: • (a) chest infection • severe exhaustion • no feeling in her feet / no feeling in her hands • serious problems breathing	4

Exercise 2

Question	Answer	Marks
10(a)	C	1
10(b)	D	1
10(c)	A	1
10(d)	C	1
10(e)	A	1
10(f)	B	1
10(g)	C	1
10(h)	D	1
10(i)	A	1
10(j)	B	1

Exercise 3

Question	Answer	Marks
11	1 mark for each acceptable response, up to a maximum of 4 marks: • (a small) increase in (the) size of (the) balls • (the) ball (now) moves (through the air a little) more slowly / easier (for people watching) to see (what was happening) • more (variety of) playing styles • (much) better analysis of opponents (before matches)	4

Question	Answer	Marks
12	1 mark for each acceptable response, up to a maximum of 3 marks: • (far) more people play table tennis there • (their) table tennis facilities are excellent • kids (there) start playing (table tennis very) young • (very) advanced training methods	3
13	1 mark for each acceptable response, up to a maximum of 2 marks: • have several balls (available) for players (to use) • fewer breaks • stricter rules about (the) rubber covers on (the players') bats	2

Exercise 4

Question	Answer	Marks
14	Relevant points to include: • start (with) a project on a particular subject • look for wildlife at dawn / look for wildlife at dusk • think (carefully) about (the) light • check the weather forecast • do (some) research (into the animal's behaviour) • take photos from the same eye level as the animal • think about the background • tell a story in a photo • keep trying • experiment with different camera settings	8

Exercise 5

Sample answer A

> Hello my friend Hassan
>
> This Ahmed. Long time don't see you. May be last two years. I miss you my friend. My life is OK. I study a lot the maths and science. I don't like other subjects. I think you know I'm terrible for languages and history. My family move another house. It is big the old house. Now I have my own bedroom. My brother is too. OK Hassan I want see you soon. Long time didn't see you. We can talk many things. Do you go holiday this year? I think this year my family go Lebanon for holiday. You can meet me in the mall? You tell me when.
>
> Your friend
>
> Ahmed

(116 words)

Comments

Content: The task is only partially fulfilled because the first point (ask for some information about your friend's life in the last two years) is not addressed. The second point is dealt with and the third point is answered briefly, but at 116 words, the email is under the required length. The style is appropriate for a friend and it is clear who the writer is writing to and why.

Language: Some common vocabulary is used appropriately but the range of vocabulary is limited. The structures used are simple with no complex sentences. There are grammatical errors in almost every sentence including the use of verb tenses and forms, prepositions, word order in questions and missing articles. There are no linking words so the text doesn't flow at all, and there is no attempt at paragraphing. The meaning is sometimes unclear and control of language and organisation is limited.

Marks: Content 3
        Language 2

Sample answer B

> Hi Viktor
>
> I'm Maxim, your old friend from school. I found your email address and I decided to write to you.
>
> We don't see each other really long time. I know that you moved to another house and another school. How is your life now? And your new school? And your family?
>
> I'm still in the same school with the same friends. Do you remember Pavel, Sergei and Yury? We still playing volleyball together every week. Last year, I started to play

chess a lot and now I'm in school chess team. In fact, I think I'm more chess player than the sportsman.

> Do you remember my sister Natasha? She finished the school and she is now at the university study law because she wants to be lawyer. She loves the university.
>
> Viktor, do you think you will come here one day? I know that your aunt and cousin still living near here so maybe one day you will visit them. If you come, it will be great to meet up. We can have coffee together and tell the news of our lives. Maybe we play volleyball with our old friends.
>
> Just let me know.
>
> Your friend Maxim

(198 words)

Comments

Content: All three points are clearly covered so the task is fulfilled. The style is appropriate and the writer is very clear about why he is writing and who he is writing to. The content is developed and the length is appropriate. The message is generally communicated effectively.

Language: There is a good range of common vocabulary used appropriately. Simple structures are used effectively, and there are a number of complex sentences. There are a few grammatical errors, mainly in the use of articles, but also in tense use. However, the meaning is always clear. The text is well-organised with effective paragraphing and linking between sentences.

Marks: Content 7
        Language 5

Exercise 6

Sample answer A

> Every year the City Summer Music Festival has a great selection of concerts featuring classical music, jazz, folk, rock and hip-hop, and also music from different parts of the world.
>
> This year I saw a band called 'Tinariwen' from north Africa. I never heard of them before but my dad had tickets and persuaded me in going with him. I'm very glad I went. There were eight musicians on the stage including two women singers, two guitarists, a bass player, a keyboard player, a drummer and a man who played several different instruments.
>
> Dressed in beautiful traditional clothes from north Africa, they mainly sang in own Tuareg language, but also sometimes in French, I think. Although I didn't understand any of the words, I loved their sound. I'm not sure what kind of music I expected them to play, but it was very

different from <u>anything I never heard before</u>. Apparently, it's called 'desert blues' and it sounds like a mixture of traditional north Africa music and American blues. To my ears it's a great sound. It's not party music – in fact, a lot of the singing sounds very sad – but it's got great rhythm. If you ever get the chance to see this band, I'd definitely recommend it.

(209 words)

Comments

Content: The task is fulfilled well. The style is consistently appropriate, and there is an adequate sense of purpose and audience. The description of the concert is well-developed and the content is communicated skilfully and effectively. The length is slightly over the upper word limit.

Language: A wide range of common and less common vocabulary is used effectively. Both simple and more complex structures are used appropriately and accurately. There are a few minor errors which do not affect understanding. The text is well-organised, and there is effective linking.

Marks: Content 8
       Language 8

Sample answer B

Hi Kelly

I want to tell you about the 'Lucky Boys' concert I went to yesterday. I think you know that they are my favourite band. I have all the songs on my phone but <u>I never hear them in live before</u>. They are the best. <u>I think I tell you before that my favourite singer in the group is Sean he's from Australia but I like the other four too Paddy, Kieran, Joe and Finn.</u> I think there were 3000 fans there last night and everyone was really excited. Actually 80% of the fans were girls and <u>we all made much noise</u>. In fact we screamed because <u>we are so excited</u>. The singing was <u>fantastic just like on the recordings and</u> the dancing was great too. In some of the songs the groups asked everyone in the audience <u>to sing with them that was fantastic</u>. I never sing so loud in my life. Today I'm very tired and my voice is not good but <u>I'm so happy for going to the concert</u>. The next time the Lucky Boys come here you must go to see them with me.

See you soon

xxxx

Emma

(194 words)

Comments

Content: The task is partially fulfilled. A concert is described with some development and detail, but it is in the form of an email to a friend rather than a review for a magazine. There is a sense of purpose and audience, but in the wrong genre. The length is appropriate and the content is communicated effectively.

Language: Common vocabulary is used, mostly appropriately. A good range of simple structures is used appropriately, and there are some complex structures. There are some errors with the use of verbs forms and tenses, verb patterns and punctuation. The punctuation errors may cause some initial difficulties for a reader, but the meaning is mostly clear. The text would be more accessible if it was divided into paragraphs.

Marks: Content 5
       Language 5

Practice Test 4

Listening

Exercise 1

Question	Answer	Marks
1(a)	(the) volleyball team	1
1(b)	kindness (to others)	1
2(a)	time keeping	1
2(b)	(too) ambitious	1
3(a)	(the) brakes	1
3(b)	(the) swimming pool	1
4(a)	(its) (astonishing) speed	1
4(b)	rabbits	1

Exercise 2

Question	Answer	Marks
5(i)	peas	1
5(ii)	digging	1
5(iii)	frost	1
5(iv)	kitchen waste	1
5(v)	pond	1
5(vi)	greenhouse	1
5(vii)	herb	1
5(viii)	landscape gardener	1

Exercise 3

Question	Answer	Marks
6(i)	D	1
6(ii)	G	1
6(iii)	B	1
6(iv)	E	1
6(v)	F	1
6(vi)	A	1

Exercise 4

Question	Answer	Marks
7(a)	C	1
7(b)	B	1
7(c)	B	1
7(d)	A	1
7(e)	C	1
7(f)	A	1
7(g)	C	1
7(h)	A	1

Exercise 5

Question	Answer	Marks
8(a)(i)	mechanical puzzles	1
8(a)(ii)	board games	1
8(a)(iii)	medicine	1
8(a)(iv)	construction sets	1
8(a)(v)	action figures	1
8(b)(i)	chess	1
8(b)(ii)	wood	1
8(b)(iii)	space rocket	1
8(b)(iv)	Little Professor / little professor	1
8(b)(v)	safety regulations	1